The Complete Guide to Golden Retrievers

Dr. Jo de Klerk

LP Media Inc. Publishing

Text copyright © 2019 by LP Media Inc.

www.lpmedia.org

Publication Data

Dr. Jo de Klerk

The Complete Guide to Golden Retrievers ---- First edition.

Summary: "Successfully raising a Golden Retriever dog from puppy to old age" --- Provided by publisher.

ISBN: 978-1-79748-554-6

[1. Golden Retriever --- Non-Fiction] I. Title.

Design by Sorin Rădulescu

First paperback edition, 2019

TABLE OF CONTENTS

CHAPTER 16

THE COMPLETE GUIDE TO GOLDEN RETRIEVERS
By Dr. Jo de Klerk

Golden Retrievers are one of the most loyal and lovable breeds around, and it is easy to see why they are so popular. They are playful and friendly, even into their golden years, and are ideal dogs for first-time dog owners. This book provides all you need to know about the breed, whether you are buying a Golden Retriever for a pet, working dog, show dog, or breeding dog.

In The Complete Guide to Golden Retrievers you will learn everything you need to know from start to end; how to choose a puppy, training, traveling, grooming, health care, and senior care. You will also learn all about the background of the breed, its history, breed predisposed diseases, and special traits. All the information is specific to Golden Retrievers and in easy-to-read, comprehensive detail.

Whether you are a veteran Golden Retriever owner or new to the breed, there will be something for everyone in this book.

Compiled by veterinarian Dr. Jo de Klerk, this book will ensure there is nothing left for you to wonder or worry about. It will provide you with everything you need to know to help you care for, train, and bond with your new lovable friend.

CHAPTER 1
Breed Overview

It's no surprise that the Golden Retriever is one of the world's most popular dogs. Both beautiful and intelligent, the Golden Retriever fits right into family life, despite being bred originally as a working dog. This shows how adaptable the breed is, and how bonded a Golden Retriever can become to its human pack. If you are thinking of welcoming a Golden Retriever into your home, this book will take you through all the basics of understanding the breed and knowing how to meet your dog's needs.

Photo Courtesy of Meghan Shoeman

About the Breed

The Golden Retriever is instantly recognizable, but often confused with the Labrador Retriever. Both breeds have their origins in the same broad gene pool, with a common ancestor in the Saint John's Dog of Newfoundland. And both have water dogs amongst their ancestors, being bred as working dogs to retrieve fallen game from marshy terrain. Both breeds are also exceptionally intelligent, friendly, water-loving, and keen on their food. And both make superb family dogs. There are, however, a few characteristics of the Golden Retriever that distinguish him from his Labrador cousin.

Looks

The Golden Retriever, as the name suggests, comes in only one color, and that is golden. There may be some variation in shade within the breed from almost white to caramel, but unlike the Labrador, which comes in golden, chocolate, and black, these broad variations are not seen in the Golden Retriever. Also, as a descendant of the wavy-coated Retriever, the Golden boasts a luxuriant long coat compared to his Labrador cousin's flat coat.

FUN FACT

Popular Pals

According to the American Kennel Club (AKC), Golden Retrievers are the third most popular breed in the United States.

Generally speaking, the Labrador is bigger than the Golden Retriever, although by a slim margin, so size anomalies can make this an unreliable distinction. Females are smaller than males. Male Golden Retrievers typically are 23 to 24 inches tall and weigh 65 to 75 pounds. Females are generally 21.5 to 22.5 inches tall and 55 to 65 pounds. Goldens have soft mouths for retrieving game undamaged, and a characteristic smile that gives them an appealing, friendly appearance.

The appearance of the Golden Retriever differs slightly between countries, as the breed standard is not exactly the same in every country, and as a pedigree dog, Golden Retrievers should be bred in strict adherence to the breed standard of their country.

The Golden Retriever in America may be darker in color than his British counterpart. The British Golden is stockier than his American cousin, with a broader head. He may also be slightly larger.

The Golden Retriever boasts some beautiful feathering around his neck, belly, the backs of his legs, and the underside of his tail. His coat really is his crowning glory and something that draws many people to the breed. It is, however, high maintenance compared to the Labrador's flat coat, so the prospective owner needs to commit to regular grooming. Allergy sufferers will not do well with this breed as the coat sheds profusely.

The stunning good looks of the Golden Retriever have made it a favorite across the world, and a popular star in the media, and it is not hard to see why.

Photo Courtesy of Ashley DeFrancesco

Age Expectancy

The typical lifespan of a Golden Retriever is 10-12 years. When taking on a Golden Retriever puppy, it is important to think ahead and consider any changes in your personal circumstances that may occur over this period, and whether you can commit to your dog's care for the whole of its life.

A few decades ago, Golden Retrievers might have been expected to live up to 16 or 17 years. Studies are currently being carried out into why the average lifespan has dropped so dramatically in recent years. These studies are considering environmental factors, lifestyle changes, genes, and health conditions. However, as no conclusions have yet been reached, all you can do as an owner is ensure your dog has a good diet, is kept at a healthy weight, has plenty of exercise, and receives regular veterinary care to ensure he lives his allotted years to the maximum.

Personality

Quite simply, the Golden Retriever is one huge personality on four legs with a waggy tail. Nothing sets the Golden Retriever apart so much as his friendly, sunny nature, his huge smile, and his gentle, devoted nature. Your Golden Retriever will love you unconditionally, trust you implicitly, and forgive all your mistakes. Every day is his best day ever, and he will love to be a part of your family, joining in with all your activities and enthusiastically welcoming every visitor to your home.

A word you will come across regularly in this book is "biddable." This is the characteristic set out in the official breed standard to describe the personality of the Golden Retriever, and it means your dog is eager to please and follow your instructions. It also implies that the Golden Retriever is shaped both by his nature and by the training you do with him. So, in terms of the raw material, you have an ideal foundation in a well-bred Golden Retriever, but there is still work to do to create the perfect dog.

Chapter 3 of this book looks at the behavior of a Golden Retriever, and notes that although there is an accepted standard personality for the breed, variations may occur due to genetics. For example, working lines will be more high-energy. Also, character anomalies can occur even between litter-mates that can be unpredictable. Additionally, if you are adopting an older dog from a rescue, his early experiences may have been damaging to his personality, and there will be work to do in regaining his trust and restoring to him his natural demeanor. Sadly, some damaged dogs may never achieve emotional well-being after being mistreated or neglected. The Golden Retriever is a resilient and forgiving breed by nature, however so the chances are better than average.

If your Golden Retriever doesn't completely fill your home and your life on account of his size, his huge personality certainly will! You will never have a dull day in all the years you get to spend in the company of a Golden Retriever.

Inside the Home

The Golden Retriever is a large dog. It goes without saying that the small bundle of fluff you bring home as a puppy will rapidly grow into a large and exuberant adult dog, with a long waggy tail capable of clearing a coffee table with one sweep. So, the very first consideration you have to face in deciding whether this is the breed for you is, just how big is your house and the rooms within it?

If you are living alone and this is unlikely to change, you may find ample space in a modestly sized home for yourself and your large friend. If you have a large family, however, you need to think about the space a Golden Retriever will occupy. Of course, your dog does not necessarily have to have access to the whole house, as long as the rooms he is allowed to occupy are large enough and free from hazards. This is a matter of personal preference and there are no hard and fast rules, as long as careful thought has been given to the impact that a large, energetic dog will have on the household before he makes his home with you.

The Golden Retriever is known to be a profuse shedder, so if you are particularly house proud, you may have to lower your standards in welcoming a Golden into your home, unless you want to spend a lot of extra time with the vacuum cleaner! Certain textiles will attract and retain hair, whereas hard surfaces and leather or vinyl upholstery will be easier to maintain in a house shared with a Golden Retriever. Generally, these

Photo Courtesy of
Linda Walkowiak

surfaces are also easier to clean during the housebreaking stage with your dog, so there are always some practicalities to consider which may make your life easier if the Golden Retriever is the breed for you.

Unfortunately for some, a Golden will never be an option, since with its thick, shedding undercoat and silky top coat, the breed is not suitable for severe allergy sufferers. You may also wish to consider whether any regular visitors to your home, such as extended family, are allergic to dogs before settling on a Golden Retriever.

The Golden Retriever is known to carry with it a distinctive doggy odor. To many people this is not a problem in the least and even rather endearing, but if it is likely to offend you, then you may reconsider your choice of a Golden Retriever as that is just his natural perfume. Dogs should not be bathed excessively as it strips the coat of its natural oils, and doggy deodorants are not recommended. Over time, as an owner, you will become nose-blind to your dog, but if you are concerned that your house smells doggy to visitors then a Golden may not be the breed for you.

If you have weighed the pros and cons of the impact a Golden Retriever will have on your home, and decided that you have the space, you are relaxed about dog hair, drool, and odor and have some strategies in place to minimize this, then there is no doubt that your home will be complete with a Golden always ready to welcome you at the door and put the day's troubles back into perspective!

Outside the Home

If you are considering a Golden Retriever, it is important that you either have your own back yard or access to a safe space immediately outside your home for the dog to use for regular toileting. A private back yard is obviously preferable because you can make it secure to enable your dog to have regular access to a relaxing outside space where he may be off lead and enjoy the sunshine. For a large dog such as a Golden, the home itself may feel confining even if he is taken for regular exercise, so he will enjoy a secure yard.

You should always ensure your yard fence is high enough to prevent your Golden from jumping out, and that it goes right to the ground if you have a puppy. Puppies in any case should be supervised outdoors as they may dig and eat inappropriate items or plants. If you are adopting a dog from a shelter, the home checker will cast an experienced eye over your outdoor space and make suggestions if they see any shortcomings such as broken fence panels, other escape routes, or hazardous objects. These will need to be attended to before you can bring your rescue dog home. But if you are buying a puppy and have never had a dog before, it may be worth asking an experienced dog owning friend to check your yard. If you have a pool or pond, you should fence it off before your dog arrives. Further advice in preparing your home and yard may be found in Chapter 5.

Your Golden Retriever will also enjoy ownership of his wider territory, including his regular walks, whether these may be accessed on foot from your home, or via a short car journey. Although it is nice for your dog to enjoy a wide variety of walks, he will always appreciate his special places that he knows well, and where all his favorite scents are in the expected places. If you live in town, you should try to make time to drive out to the countryside or the ocean on a regular basis for your Golden Retriever, because adaptable as he is, he was bred as a working dog and will only be able to exercise his natural instincts in a more rural environment. Be aware, however, of dangers such as strong ocean currents, fast-flowing rivers, and steep cliff faces, and use a lead where your dog's enthusiasm may get him into trouble. Make sure your dog has an identity tag on his collar and is microchipped with your up-to-date contact details in case he should stray.

Costs of Keeping a Golden Retriever

The most immediate cost involved when acquiring a Golden Retriever is the price of the dog, and as a Golden is a pedigree breed, this will be quite high. On average you may expect to pay $500-$2,000 for a Golden Retriever with documented bloodlines. While you may pick up a dog for a lower price, be aware that an undocumented dog may have been bred with little regard for the breed standard or the suitability of the parents, and may turn out to have more health issues further down the road. You may alternatively be taking on a rescue dog from a shelter, but these dogs are not free; you will always need to pay a rehoming fee. This may be in the region of $200-$500 and goes to cover the general costs the rescue incurs in their work, such as neutering, vaccinations, microchipping, fostering, accommodation, feeding, transport, and administration. It also ensures no one regards a rescue as a place to pick up a free dog for illegal dog fighting, breeding, or selling on.

Golden Retrievers are quite costly dogs to keep on account of their size and potential health issues. Preventative veterinary medicine is discussed in Chapter 11, and insurance for veterinary fees is strongly recommended from the outset, since the sorts of ailments to which a Golden Retriever is predisposed are potentially very costly. Alternatively, some owners prefer to self-insure, where they put aside a regular amount for unforeseen veterinary costs. This is a matter of preference, although operations can run into thousands of dollars, and faced with the cost of an expensive procedure that may not be successful, owners that do not have insurance are faced with an unenviable choice, or no choice at all other than euthanasia if they do not have the funds in place.

On a more regular basis, the cost of feeding your Golden Retriever will be higher than average because he is a large dog. Also because of his genetic predisposition to joint issues and other health problems in later life, you will want to be sure he is on a high-quality diet. Nutrition is discussed in Chapter 8, and once you have an idea which type of food you want for your dog, it is worth looking up the recommended quantities for an adult-weight Golden (55-75 pounds), calculating the number of portions in the bag, the number of cans per day, or the volume of raw meat if this is your preference, and working out what feeding your dog will cost you month by month. Don't forget your dog deserves a treat from time to time, especially in the course of his training, so build a little into the budget for this as well.

One expense that needs to be considered during the second year of your puppy's life is the cost of neutering your dog. This is recommended if you do not plan to show or breed from your dog, as it will prevent un-

Photo Courtesy of
Curtis McCollough

wanted pregnancies, eliminate seasons in the female, and also help your dog to be more settled. Golden Retrievers, however, are one of a few breeds that should not be neutered before one year of age, as they require the effect of hormones to close the long-bone growth plates. If you decide to neuter your dog, this should ideally be between 1 and 2 years in a Golden Retriever.

Apart from one-off costs such as neutering, you will also have other regular costs such as parasite treatments and annual vaccinations which should figure in the budget.

The equipment you will need for your dog mostly comprises a high initial cost, with smaller expenses along the way as your dog outgrows, wears out, or destroys his bedding, crate, harness, toys, leashes, etc. An idea of what you will need for your new dog is given in Chapter 5. After the initial outlay, you will be more at leisure to look for bargains or secondhand items when replacement becomes necessary if you are on a budget. For many owners, however, indulging their dog gives them a lot of pleasure, so again this is a matter of personal choice.

The activities you choose to participate in with your dog may vary wildly in cost. For many owners, it is sufficient just to socialize their dog informally and train him themselves using online tutorials or past experience. They may have easy access to the countryside or local parks for walks, and never need to spend a cent on entertaining their dog. Other owners, however, may like the idea of formal puppy socialization classes and dog training classes, for the moral and practical support this brings, and the chance to mix with and learn from other dog owners. Also, many owners like the idea of Agility classes and Flyball sessions. Most of these group classes will involve a fee and possibly some additional equipment. If you plan to compete at a higher level there will also be additional costs. The highest costs of all in the "optional" category are incurred if you wish to show your dog. In this case you will be prepared for entry fees, travel costs, and all the expenses involved in keeping your dog in tiptop cosmetic condition. These are discussed in Chapter 15.

So as a general rule, keeping a Golden Retriever is costlier than the average dog. However, as with any dog, a lot of the expenses are optional, and you can keep the costs down, so the choice of a Golden Retriever does not have to exclude those on lower incomes, as long as present and future expenses have been budgeted for. Quite simply, your dog has no concept of wealth; all that matters to him is that he is comfortable, adequately fed, well exercised, free from pain, and has human company for a good portion of the day, with the opportunity to meet friends of his own species as well. If you can guarantee him these basic requirements then you will both enjoy a relationship that is second to none!

CHAPTER 2
Breed History

"The Golden Retriever breed standard speaks of a dog that is trust-worthy and friendly, never 'quarrelsome 'under normal conditions. A golden was a gentleman's hunting dog, and should be both beautiful and athletic."

Jill Simmons
PoeticGold Farm

Origin of the Breed

Photo Courtesy of Stephanie Johnston

The Golden Retriever owes its existence as a breed to Dudley Majoribanks, Lord Tweedmouth, who lived at Guisachan House in the Inverness Highlands of Scotland in the late 1800s. The Highlands were the traditional hunting grounds of the United Kingdom, but the landscape was pocketed with marshes and rivers, so sportsmen required a breed of retriever that could work over all terrains to retrieve both upland game and waterfowl. In addition, longer-range firearms had led to game being shot at a greater distance, so a breed with excellent stamina capable of working at a further range was required.

Genetics

The ancestor of the Golden Retriever was known as the wavy-coated retriever, whose origins go back to the Saint John's Dog of Newfoundland, which is also the ancestor of the Labrador Retriever. In 1865, Dudley Majoribanks purchased a young yellow wavy-coated retriever from a cobbler in Brighton, on the south coast of England. The cobbler had acquired the puppy the previous year from the gamekeeper of the local landowner, Lord Chichester, in payment of a debt, and was the only yellow puppy from a litter of black wavy-coated retrievers. The dog was named Nous, which means "wisdom," and was clearly a dog of great quality to attract Majoribanks' attention. Nous was taken back to Guisachan in Scotland to join his kennel of sporting dogs and become the sire of a new breed.

> **FUN FACT**
> **Lord Tweedmouth**
> **Developed the Bree**
>
> Dudley Marjoribanks, also known as Lord Tweedmouth, developed the Golden Retriever from 1840 to 1890 because he wanted a gundog that would retrieve birds from both land and water. He crossed a "Yellow Retriever" with the now-extinct Tweed Water Spaniel and added some Bloodhound and Irish Setter to the mix to eventually create the Golden Retriever as we know it today.

Another breed of hunting dog in Dudley Majoribanks' kennels was the Tweed Water Spaniel, which is a breed that is now extinct, but as its name suggests had the ability to retrieve game from water, with a soft mouth to carry it undamaged. Nous was bred to a Tweed Water Spaniel named Belle in 1868 and 1871, and the resulting yellow puppies became the foundation for a new and distinct line of yellow retrievers.

Thanks to meticulous records kept by Dudley Majoribanks in a journal from 1840 to 1890, the development of the breed now known as the Golden Retriever was documented, and these kennel records are now in the UK Kennel Club library. Through careful line breeding from Nous and Belle's descendants with other wavy and flat-coated retrievers, another Tweed Water Spaniel, a Red Setter, and possibly a Labrador Retriever and a Bloodhound, the breed was developed. The yellow retrievers were generally kept by Majoribanks to continue the line, but he also retained a few of the black puppies. Many of the dogs bred by Majoribanks were given to friends and family as working gundogs. Whereas today the Golden Retriever has found a role as a family pet, working ability was paramount at this stage in the breed's development with an emphasis on exceptional water capabilities.

Historical Standards

Up until the early twentieth century, Majoribanks' new breed of hunting dog was little known anywhere other than the Scottish Highlands, but in 1904, one of Majoribanks' dogs won the first field trial for retrievers and came to wider notice, and a few years later the breed was being shown at dog shows. They were still known at this stage as Yellow Retrievers. In 1908, Lord Harcourt of Nuneham Park in Oxford, who had developed a liking for the breed, gathered a collection of retrievers from the original matings and entered them at the Kennel Club show. They were entered under the class "Any Variety Retriever" as "Yellow Flatcoated Retrievers"; however, the interest generated by Lord Harcourt's dogs led to them being described for the first time as "Golden Retrievers," and by the time they were registered in their own right with the Kennel Club of England in 1911, they acquired the classification "Retriever – Yellow or Golden." It was in 1920 that they were officially classified as "Retriever – Golden" by the British Kennel Club, being recognized by the Canadian Kennel Club in 1925 and the American Kennel Club in 1932.

Photo Courtesy of Samantha Hector

One misconception about the origin of the Golden Retriever is that they were descended from the Russian circus dog. This came about when an early admirer of the breed, Colonel Le Poer Trench, bred a line of Goldens that he claimed were derived from Majoribanks' Guisachan lines and on the good authority of Majoribanks' own kennel man, were descended from Russian circus dogs. Col. Trench was a man of some status and con-

FUN FACT
AKC Registration

The Golden Retriever was first shown in Britain in 1908 and was first registered by the AKC in 1925.

sequently his breed that he called "Russian Retrievers" was believed to have originated in Russia. When Majoribanks' kennel notes came to light, however, this theory was debunked. However, it caused confusion at the time as well as a lasting controversy about the true origins of the breed, although Col. Trench's line may be considered purer than the Goldens developed by Majoribanks, as they were never crossbred from the original strain.

Photo Courtesy of Leslie Jenkins

In the early days of showing in the UK, Golden Retrievers had to compete against Col. Le Poer Trench's Yellow Russian Retrievers for Challenge Certificates, as although they had separate classes, they were only assigned one set of Challenge Certificates, which the Russian Retrievers won. When the Goldens were assigned their own Challenge Certificates, however, the first winners were Mrs. Charlesworth's dog Noranby Sandy and Mr. F.W. Herbert's bitch Coquette. Mrs. Charlesworth then went on to win three Challenge Certificates and a Field Trial with Noranby Campfire. A suspension of canine activities during the First World War drew things to a halt, but the Golden Retriever was by now established in the affections of the public.

The Golden Retriever first came to the United States in the early twentieth century and was an instant hit. The most notable foundation sire was born in England in 1929 and called Am/Can Ch Speedwell Pluto, imported by Samuel S. Magoffin of North Vancouver as his personal gundog. Speedwell Pluto became an AKC champion, the first Golden to win a Sporting Group, and the first to go Best in Show. Samuel Magoffin and his brother John Rogers Magoffin imported further well-bred bitches from England for their Rockhaven and Gilnockie kennels, and became the foundation for the Golden Retriever breed in the American West and Midwest.

Initially when the breed standard had been drawn up in 1911, cream had been excluded as a permissible color, and was not popular in the 1920s, with the darker shades being more widely favored. However, in the 1930s, the lighter shades gained a resurgence in popularity, and in 1936 the UK breed standard was altered to include "Any shade of gold or cream, but neither red or mahogany," as this was seen to be more aligned to the original Guisachan breeding.

As the breed continued to develop on a much wider basis throughout the twentieth century, certain deviations began to creep in that began to cause concern. The tall, setter look was seen more in mid-century shows, and certain health concerns such as overshot or undershot bites and eyelid issues were not being addressed. Consequently in 1955, the old AKC breed standard was revised, disqualifying dogs with incorrect dentition, abnormal eyelash position, and those outside of a stricter height limit.

At this time, the breed standards between the UK and the US began to diverge, with the lighter-colored, square-set dogs being favored in the British Isles, in contrast to the darker, lankier American Golden Retriever.

As the breed has been refined and developed, organizations such as the Golden Retriever Club of America and the Golden Retriever Breed Council in the UK have acted to ensure that the health of the breed remains paramount.

Photo Courtesy of
Claire Moody

Famous Golden Retrievers in History

Photo Courtesy of
Kristin Stohl-Carlson

American President Gerald R. Ford was very partial to Golden Retrievers. The Fords' third Golden, Liberty, was given to them by their daughter Susan while Ford was serving as President, and as a consequence became a resident of the Oval Office, with swimming rights in the pool at Camp David and lounging privileges on the South Lawn of the White House. Liberty also helped to keep a sense of perspective in the Oval Office, being trained to end awkward conversations by a signal from her master to approach the visitor wagging her tail. It could be said that every presidential office needs a Golden Retriever to make the world a better place.

This sentiment was clearly echoed by President Ronald Reagan, whose caramel-colored Golden Retriever, Victory, was given to him in 1980 during his campaign trail on the proviso that it would be cared for until he entered the White House. On winning the election, Victory became First Dog; however, he didn't move to the White House, as the Reagans thought their ranch in California was a more suitable place for him, where he always welcomed them on their vacations, accompanying the President on ranch work and out horseback riding.

Not to be outdone, other nations' leaders have owned Golden Retrievers, including Aldo, owned by Russian President Dmitry Medvedev, and Abby, owned by Australian Prime Minister Kevin Rudd and who was also featured in a children's book written by the Premier, Jasper and Abby and the Great Australia Day Kerfuffle.

In the UK, Children's TV presenter Simon Groom had a Golden Retriever named Goldie, who appeared on Blue Peter from 1978 to 1986. Goldie's puppy Bonnie became her successor, imprinting the breed's happy-natured appeal on a generation of British children.

Golden Retrievers are so intelligent, trainable, and photogenic that they are natural film stars. Basketball-playing Buddy was the star of the movie Air Bud in 1997. He also played the role of Comet in the TV sitcom Full House.

Homeward Bound: The Incredible Journey (1993) and its sequel, Homeward Bound: Lost in San Francisco (1996) featured a cat and two dogs, one of which was a Golden Retriever, Shadow (voiced by Don Ameche). Shadow was mainly played by Ben, with three other body doubles, and the dogs on set were paid in liver treats. Although Golden Retrievers are extremely trainable, one clue that the words are voiced is the fact that none of the animals' mouths move when they speak!

It's hardly surprising that Golden Retrievers are a hit with celebrities, and no doubt provide a leveling and calming influence in their hectic lives. Celebrities who have owned Golden Retrievers include Indira Gandhi, Jackie Chan, Sally Field, Enrique Iglesias, Tom Cruise, Sheryl Crow, Joe Cocker, Jamie Lee Curtis, Paul Newman, Neil Diamond, Oprah Winfrey, Pamela Anderson, Mary Tyler Moore, and many more. Christopher Reeve owned a Golden Retriever as an assistance dog.

From its early origins, bred and developed within the confines of Dudley Majoribanks' Scottish estate as a working dog, the Golden Retriever has grown to become one of the world's most popular and recognized breeds, equally at home in front of the fire as out in the field. They are not a breed to be taken on lightly, however, and a little understanding of their background will help any prospective owner decide if the Golden Retriever is the right dog for their lifestyle and circumstances. When it all comes together, owning a Golden Retriever (or, as many would say, being owned by a Golden Retriever) is a mutually rewarding partnership for life.

CHAPTER 3
Behavior

Temperament

The characteristic that defines the Golden Retriever above all else is its friendly, loyal, sunny, and biddable temperament. This is down to the long history of careful, selective breeding, and the stringent adherence to the breed standards. In producing an instantly recognizable appearance, selective breeding should also produce a certain uniformity of temperament, and broadly speaking this is the case. You can expect a Golden Retriever to be gentle, loyal, happy, and safe around adults, children, and other animals. However, anomalies of temperament can occur, and it is important to acknowledge these.

Photo Courtesy of
Lori Reuter – Avalor Goldens

Photo Courtesy of
Julie & Holly Simmons
PrairieWyn Golden Retrievers

Firstly, you may reasonably assume that a litter of puppies will be genetically predisposed to the temperament of the parents. In the ideal breeding situation, both parents will be proven to be of excellent temperament, conforming to the breed standard:

Temperament: Friendly, reliable, and trustworthy. Quarrelsomeness or hostility towards other dogs or people in normal situations, or an unwarranted show of timidity or nervousness, is not in keeping with Golden Retriever character. (AKC Breed Standard 1990)

Temperament: Kindly, friendly and confident. (British Kennel Club 1994)

Anomalies in temperament may occur when two Golden Retrievers are mated that are not of similar temperaments, in which case the puppies may inherit either parent's character traits. Or occasionally, genetics are just unpredictable, and for no clear reason, an atypical temperament may occur in a random pup from the litter. It is important that dogs inheriting a temperament that does not conform to the breed standard should not be bred, in order to preserve the hallmark biddable temperament of the Golden Retriever.

Temperament may also be affected by unfortunate experiences in the early life of a dog. Cruelty or just poor training may result in behavioral issues that may or may not be overcome later in more experienced hands.

It is also important to be aware that despite the Golden Retriever's well-deserved reputation as the perfect family dog, a veterinary survey in the 1990s listed the breed among the top ten of dogs that bite. This is certainly not a typical breed characteristic but indicates that careful research should be done by the prospective owner into the pedigree of the dog they intend to bring into their home, especially if they have young children. Equally, early training and socialization are paramount, as Goldens that bite are most likely to have suffered a poor experience in the critical first few months of life.

Trainability

"Most Goldens are very easy to train and want to please, and interact with their people. I always suggest a good puppy obedience class to get both the owner and puppy started in the right direction."

Julie Simmons
PrairieWyn Golden Retrievers

Golden Retrievers are renowned for their exceptional intelligence and eagerness to please. This makes them very trainable, to the extent that they are commonly used as assistance dogs and in search and rescue. They were of course originally bred as working dogs, so from their very origins were expected to learn and respond to commands. Naturally, this doesn't mean your Golden Retriever is born knowing how to sit, stay, and heel, or that toileting should take place outdoors. Teaching these things is all part of the bonding process with your new dog. But you may have high expectations for your Golden Retriever, and enjoy the rewards of training a dog that is quick to learn, and adaptable to life within its human pack.

Some basic commands will be discussed in Chapter 6, but your Golden Retriever is capable of learning at a very high level, which is one of the attributes of the breed that makes them almost human.

Photo Courtesy of
Marnie Harrell
Shadymist Kennel, LLC

Photo Courtesy of David A Ring

Separation Anxiety

The very fact that your Golden Retriever is so bonded to his humans means that the breed is especially susceptible to separation anxiety, as he cannot bear to be away from the people that are his world. However, your Golden Retriever is a large breed dog when fully grown, inclined to molt and drool and fill any confined space he may find himself in. Therefore, he is not portable like smaller breeds and there will be occasions he has to stay at home. It is important to condition your dog to this necessary requirement from an early age, so he knows you will be coming back, and he feels comfortable and safe alone in his home environment.

Of course, if you have the space, you may consider another dog as a companion for your Golden, but this is a luxury not all will be able to accommodate. Your intelligent Golden Retriever may also not consider the other dog any substitute for his human.

The following symptoms may be displayed by your dog if he is experiencing separation anxiety:

- Excessive drooling
- Pacing
- Barking

- Whining
- Scratching at doors
- Destroying objects such as toys or furniture

Apart from the upsetting aspect of your dog experiencing distress, the destructive elements can lead to self-trauma, particularly the claws, paws, and mouth. Consequently, separation anxiety is something you need to address if it affects your dog.

Neither punishment nor positive reward are suitable methods to reduce anxiety in your dog, as both will worsen it. However, there are some good tips which will help to gradually teach your dog that separation is not the end of the world.

When you leave your dog alone, don't make a big fuss saying goodbye. This will set his adrenaline racing. By ensuring you don't do this, he will remain in his usual calm state. Likewise, as you return to the house, initially ignore him. Greeting him and making a fuss will reinforce his anxiety. When he has calmed down after a few minutes, you can calmly say hello.

Before you leave the house, many owners find it effective to give a long-lasting stuffed toy such as a Kong®. You can stuff it with wet dog food, pâté, or peanut butter (although check it is not one which contains xylitol as an ingredient). By having something to chew and lick, not only does this distract him, but it releases endorphins, the body's natural relaxants.

In between times, you can practice leaving so that your dog gradually stops associating it with being alone for a long time. Start with just performing your leaving routine, but not actually going anywhere. Once

Photo Courtesy of Dylan Starer

this doesn't trigger any anxiety, progress to leaving the room, but only staying on the other side of the door for a few seconds. Remember not to make a fuss over him when you come back, even if he was good. You can gradually increase the time you leave him to a few minutes. Once you've reached the hour milestone without triggering his anxiety, you shouldn't have any issues leaving for a whole morning or afternoon.

Finally, there are some natural products on the market which are designed to help your pet stay calm. These may be obtained from your vet, or as non-prescription products from a pet store:

- Pheromones: "Dog appeasing pheromone" or "DAP" is released by the mother to help calm puppies for the first 5 days after birth. DAP has been manufactured into several types of products including a plug-in diffuser, a spray, and a collar.

- Casein: Naturally occurring in the mothers' milk, casein helps relax puppies, and when ingested by adult dogs, brings back the feeling of being comforted by their mother. This is available both in a tablet form, and a dry dog biscuit.

- L-tryptophan: This increases serotonin levels in the brain. Serotonin is a naturally occurring chemical which stimulates happy feelings. However, it takes a few weeks to build up to levels which make a significant difference, so don't expect to see an immediate change. It is available both in a tablet form, and a dry dog biscuit.

If you have tried all of the above and your vet has ruled out any health issues, the next step would be to consult a dog behaviorist. The benefit of this is that they can witness exactly what is going on in your own home and give personalized advice to suit your specific situation.

Chewing

Chewing is a natural behavior. It has the positive benefit of entertaining and educating your dog, cleaning his teeth, and alleviating pain. For a young puppy with teeth coming through, chewing helps with the discomfort, just as with a human baby. It is wrong therefore to punish chewing as a misbehavior issue; the owner must rather redirect it so that it causes minimum destruction to their home and belongings.

Apart from alleviating the pain of teething, puppies are more inclined to chew indiscriminately than adult dogs because they are exploring their new world, easily bored, possibly anxious while they adjust to their new life, and they have not been trained to know what is and is not acceptable to chew on. Therefore, when bringing a puppy into the home, you must expect that things left within its reach may get destroyed, as puppies have sharp teeth from a very young age. The most sensible thing to do is to place all important or dangerous objects out of the puppy's reach. If you have young children, separating the child's toys from the puppy's may present a challenge, and at this stage of your dog's development, you may consider separating the child and the dog along with their belongings by using a playpen for either the dog or the child. Be aware that children's soft toys often have hard eyes that may be pulled out and ingested by the dog, which could cause a serious obstruction, so these should never be left where the dog might find them.

Now is the time to adopt that resolution of tidying things away in the house, especially things with harmful batteries such as the TV remote. Your kitchen trash can is also fair game for your puppy, so install it behind a cupboard door, on a worktop, or in a utility room out of bounds. Stair gates in the home can also keep your puppy contained without the barrier of a closed door.

Training your puppy to feel comfortable in a crate can be an asset, as if you have to leave your dog for a while, you will know he is not destroying the house in your absence. You can even encourage positive chewing by giving him a stuffed Kong® or deer antler to chew in his crate. If he does not have a permitted chew he may set to work on the bars or mesh of the crate itself.

Remember your Golden Retriever's innate desire to please you. If you catch him in the act of chewing something inappropriate, use a stern word and remove the object. Then immediately give him a permitted chew. He will in time recognize approved chews by their scent. Praise him when his chewing is directed appropriately, and the lesson will soon be learned.

Exercise Requirement

"Young Golden Retrievers can handle a lot of exercise. A tired puppy is a good pup! Outside walks and short runs are excellent ways to tire them out."

Lanette Wright
Wright Mountain Golden Kennels

Taking on a Golden Retriever is not something to be done lightly. This is not a sedentary breed in spite of the stereotype image of a Golden flat out in front of the fire. To reach this state of relaxed bliss, your Golden Retriever will need to have done his allotted daily exercise. For an adult dog, a brisk walk of at least one hour a day is recommended, and for Goldens from working lines which have higher energy levels, this should be increased to two hours.

A lack of commitment to the exercise needs of the Golden Retriever will have an undesired result. The dog may become full of undirected energy, destructive, vocal, and obese. The Golden Retriever is a breed that loves its food, so it needs to burn off those calories. Otherwise an overweight dog will be more highly predisposed to all the weaknesses of the breed, heart disease, diabetes, high blood pressure, and stress on their hip and elbow joints.

On the positive side, the quickest and most enjoyable way to get fit and healthy yourself is to take on the exercise needs of a Golden Retriever.

Hyperactivity

It is not in the nature of the Golden Retriever to be hyperactive; they are more often described as a doormat! However, certain bloodlines will be more hyperactive than others as they have been bred specifically as working dogs where this temperament is an asset in the field. If you find yourself the owner of a dog with hyperactive tendencies that persist beyond the naturally excitable puppy stage, you may wish to adopt some coping strategies.

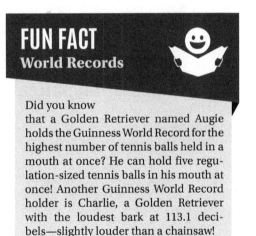

FUN FACT
World Records

Did you know that a Golden Retriever named Augie holds the Guinness World Record for the highest number of tennis balls held in a mouth at once? He can hold five regulation-sized tennis balls in his mouth at once! Another Guinness World Record holder is Charlie, a Golden Retriever with the loudest bark at 113.1 decibels—slightly louder than a chainsaw!

To begin with, you need to ask yourself if you are addressing the exercise requirement of your Golden Retriever. This is a high-energy breed, developed to be inexhaustible in the field. If you find that you have underestimated the amount of exercise your dog needs, and maybe time and work are preventing you from meeting their requirement, it may be worth employing a dog walker, or taking up an active sport with your dog, such as jogging, which will increase his mileage in a given timespan, or regular flyball or agility. Both of these will also help to exhaust his busy mind. Using your dog's natural retrieve ability by taking a ball with you to the park will also help to use up his excess energy, as will the opportunity to run and play with other dogs. It is important that strenuous exer-

FUN FACT
Fetch, Anyone?

Golden Retrievers were originally bred to retrieve birds that had been shot by hunters. Since they have an innate need to retrieve things, they'll likely want to play fetch all day!

cise should only take place after the puppy reaches the age of six months so as not to damage soft growing bones and joints. Agility and flyball may be started from nine months to one year.

Hyperactivity may also result from a dysfunction in the relationship a dog has with its human. Golden Retrievers crave attention and can become very stressed if left alone for long periods. It is important to make time for your dog. They also need a firm concept of hierarchy, and to recognize their human as the pack leader. This alleviates stress in the dog. So consistent, firm, and loving training from the outset as well as a regular routine are very important factors for your dog's mental well-being, which in turn affects his sense of calm. This understanding should help tone down unwanted hyperactivity in your Golden Retriever.

Importance of Socialization

"Never allow your puppy to interact with any animal that you don't know well! What could be worse than an innocent puppy bouncing over to another dog, or cat, only to be bitten, scratched, or worse? So make sure you keep all socialization within your control. I think the safest is a puppy class!"

Marnie J Harrell
Shadymist Kennel

Golden Retrievers are known to be very social dogs, both with humans and with other dogs. They have a special language with their own breed, however, so any opportunities to play with other Goldens is to be encouraged. Socialization is paramount for a happy, healthy dog. A dog whose life is clouded by fear of other dogs or humans may demonstrate fear aggression and stress-related health issues. Fortunately, this is not the natural disposition of a Golden Retriever, so unless you are adopting a traumatized dog, or have a dog from undesirable bloodlines, socialization should literally be a walk in the park with this breed.

There is a "Golden Window" for socializing your dog, and this is from birth to 18 weeks, during which your puppy's brain is busily processing all his new experiences. You should start socializing your Golden Retriever as soon as he arrives home. Initially this will be with human contact and exposure to unfamiliar noises, but as soon as his vaccinations are complete your dog may start puppy classes. To find out where these take place in your local area, consult your veterinarian. They may hold classes at the veterinary clinic itself; otherwise, they will be able to advise you of classes nearby. Puppy classes are an ideal way to start socialization at an early age. Your dog will have contact with other dogs and people that he does not know, and you will have support through this important stage, as well as an introduction to training classes which may be a part of the same program.

Above all, socialization should be fun for your dog. Being vigilant for when a situation might turn bad is important. Learn to recognize the body language of other dogs, and if a positive engagement does not happen within three seconds, the owner should walk their dog away before a confrontation occurs. Although a Golden is less vulnerable to attack than a small dog, emotional scars last longer than physical ones, so the owner should always be on their guard during these important early formative months.

Remember, your dog is also learning from your body language, so will pick up on your fear or anxiety. Stay upbeat, reward positive behavior, keep your dog focused, and enjoy your puppy's inquisitive journey into his new world.

Photo Courtesy of Linda Walkowiak

CHAPTER 4
How to Choose a Golden Retriever

Purchasing or Rescuing?

So, you have carefully weighed the pros and cons of sharing your life with a Golden Retriever and are ready for the commitment. The first decision you need to make is whether you are going to buy a puppy from a breeder, or a rescue from a shelter, in which case the dog will usually be an adult.

If you plan to show your dog, the second option will almost always not be open to you, because show dogs require fully papered dogs with accredited Kennel Club breeding. It is very rare for a dog with this kind of pedigree to end up in a shelter, and if it did, due perhaps to an owner handing in a dog that they could no longer care for due to a change in circumstances, then the shelter will often withhold any paperwork to protect the anonymity of the previous owner. This gives the dog a fresh start. If your showing aspirations are simply local, fun shows, then an absence of pedigree papers will be no problem, but if you had hoped to participate in Kennel Club conformation shows, these will not be open to you. In addition, shelters usually neuter dogs that pass through their care in their best interests for a settled life going forward. Neutered dogs may not participate in AKC shows, although in the UK you may apply for a "Permission to Show" letter from the Kennel Club for your neutered dog.

Show dogs also require specific training and socialization at an early age, which is covered in Chapter 15. If your rescue dog does not have this background, he may not feel comfortable in the ring, and nothing matters more when you adopt a rescue dog than to help him adjust to his new life within his comfort zone and put the past behind him.

If you plan to work your dog, again, you may find your best bet is to choose a dog carefully from specific working bloodlines. These dogs may have higher energy levels than their domestic counterparts. You will also have the opportunity to train your dog as a puppy. On the other hand, a dog from working stock that has proven too much of a handful in a family home may well end up in a shelter. In these cases, you may find a suitable dog in a shelter that will be much happier with the working life you are offering him. However, you will probably have more training to do if the dog is already an adult. But by nature, the Golden Retriever is intelli-

Photo Courtesy of Brandon Short

Photo Courtesy of Ryan Pierce

gent and wants to please, so turning such a dog around will be less of a challenge than with certain other breeds.

There is no denying that rescuing a dog brings its own sense of re-ward. In transforming the life of an unwanted dog, you are doing some-thing really positive. Also, if you would prefer to skip the puppy stage, you may be lucky enough to find a dog with basic training in place. Adopting may also suit an older person who may be looking ahead to the not too distant future when their mobility may not continue to keep pace with the needs of a Golden Retriever. Sharing a dog's twilight years is a spe-cial time. Older dogs may even come with some financial support from the rescue organization, as it is acknowledged that veterinary costs will be heavier in this chapter of their lives.

If you choose to buy a puppy, remember that a Golden Retriever is expected to live for 10-12 years, so you need to acknowledge how your life may change over this period. You will, however, have the pleasure of sharing your dog's entire lifetime with him, and he will truly become a part of the family.

Researching the Establishment

"You will want to find a breeder who does all of the health testing includ-ing hips, eyes, elbows, and hearts, as well as any additional DNA tests that are available. You should also ask questions like how are the puppies are raised, how are they socialized, and how old are they when they go home."

Angel Martin
Goldensglen Goldens

Whether you choose to purchase or rescue your Golden Retriever, you have two valuable resources available to you in finding your canine companion. These is the Kennel Club in your country, and your coun-try's Golden Retriever Club. In following up on approved establishments, whether they are breeders or shelters, you may be confident that the dog you choose will have the best chance of being healthy, and you will know you are not unwittingly supporting rogue organizations.

The most insidious trap that the prospective owner may fall into is purchasing from a puppy mill. It is common knowledge that puppy farm-ing is inhumane, that dogs are kept in unsanitary and overcrowded con-ditions, and that weakness-es are allowed to perpetuate in the stock to the extent that such dogs may end up suffer-ing or even need to be eutha-nized not long after purchase by their unsuspecting owners.

Most prospective buyers think they would never be so unaware as to purchase from a puppy mill. However, such establishments are almost al-ways fronted by a clean and tidy room in a house where the puppy is shown to the buy-er. If either of the parents are brought out, they may not even be the true parent of the pup-py. The puppy will also be un-papered if the breeder is not

Photo Courtesy of
Angie Wrightstone

HELPFUL TIP
Planning a Schedule

Golden Retrievers are extremely attached to their families and don't do well being left alone all day. If you're considering bringing a Golden into your life, try to stagger work schedules and other activities, so your Golden is never home alone for longer than six or seven hours at a time. A lonely Golden Retriever can become bored, depressed, anxious, and destructive.

approved by the Kennel Club, which should be an indicator that the dogs are not being bred from stock conforming to the breed standard. Paperwork may not seem important if you do not intend to show your dog, but Golden Retrievers are prone to many genetic health issues that responsible breeding will eliminate from the line. However cute a puppy from an unregistered breeder may look, if he is harboring genetic defects you will be guaranteed heartbreak later on, and you will be supporting reckless breeding by buying from an establishment that does not have the dog's interests at heart.

If you are rescuing a Golden Retriever from a shelter, you will find that there are several rescue organizations that exclusively cater to Labradors and Retrievers. In choosing to adopt from one of these, you will know that the establishment understands the breed, and during the time the dog has been at the rescue center, their specific needs will have been met in the most appropriate way, and any health issues addressed. Retrievers are usually fostered out during their time in rescue. This is less unsettling for the dog than spending time in kennels, and allows the rescue to assess the dog in the home environment, as well as how it reacts with children, cats, and other everyday stimuli. You should expect to pay a rehoming fee when adopting a rescue dog. This partly covers the costs of neutering, worming, vaccinating, and microchipping the dog as well as any veterinary care, accommodation, travel, and feed costs. In practice, your dog's care may have greatly exceeded this amount, and in view of the purchase cost of a pedigree dog, the rehoming fee should never be considered excessive.

On the other hand, rescue organizations can be set up by anyone, and less salubrious shelters may exist where the unfortunate dog is not assessed properly, his health needs are not addressed and may even deteriorate, and he is unlikely to be neutered, wormed, or even vaccinated. Be aware that bringing an unvaccinated rescue dog into your home may be a risk if you have other dogs. Even if you don't, losing your new rescue dog to parvovirus, which is a particular risk in puppies, is heartbreaking. While some dogs need rescuing from unscrupulous rescue organizations, there is the unfortunate aspect that such well-meaning intentions are effectively encouraging such practices to exist.

Inquire About the Parents

If you are purchasing a puppy, you will probably have viewed the litter and possibly reserved your favorite while they were still with the mother before weaning. The breeder will have been able to inform you all about the mother, her bloodlines, and her own personal health. However, the breeder may not own the sire. You may be able to make an arrangement to see him; otherwise, you will need to check out his pedigree. With both parents, research the bloodlines. Are the puppies from working stock or predominantly companion animals? Are there any past show champions in the pedigree that you can find out about? Be cautious of excessive inbreeding, where the same names crop up multiple times, especially on both parents' pedigrees. These may indicate a higher predisposition to genetic diseases. The breeder will be able to show you certification of the hip and elbow scores for both parents, which are especially important for Golden Retrievers, but what do these mean?

Hip scores:

A hip score is a measure of evidence of hip dysplasia. This is an inherited abnormal development of the hip causing instability and laxity in the joint, and the dog will be in great pain as it gets older. Hip dysplasia will not be evident in the puppy so you need to refer to the parents' hip scores to know if he is genetically predisposed to inherit the condition.

Scores range from 0 to 106, and the lower the score the better. Breeding Golden Retrievers should score below the breed median of 11.

Elbow scores:

Golden Retrievers are also susceptible to elbow dysplasia, which presents in the same way as hip dysplasia but in the forelimb and leads to osteoarthritis of the elbow joint.

An elbow score only ranges from 0-3, with 0 being clear, and 3 being badly affected. Although the two elbows may register different scores, only one number is given on the certificate, and this is the worst of the two scores. You will be looking for a score of zero in both parents to be sure your dog is not at risk of inherited elbow dysplasia.

Genetic testing:

Genetic testing for inherited disorders is a recent development in dog breeding, but it has the advantage that dogs that are carriers of certain disorders without displaying symptoms themselves may be prevented from perpetuating their genes, or only mated to dogs that present as clear. An apparently unaffected dog and bitch that both carry a recessive gene will produce offspring that suffer from the disorder. Disorders that affect Golden Retrievers that may be screened for by genetic testing include ICT-A (Ichthyosis), which is an excessively scaly skin disorder, and PRA (Progressive Retinal Atrophy), which causes blindness.

At this stage, not all Golden Retriever breeders will have carried out genetic testing on their adult dogs, but for those that have, if the results are clear it will give you the added reassurance that no nasty surprises are around the corner for your dog in later life.

Photo Courtesy of
Nathan Howland

Looking at the Puppy

So, the exciting time has come to visit the litter of puppies from which you will be choosing your new companion. This may be when the pups are around 5-7 weeks of age and not yet weaned. With a Golden Retriever, you may find it very hard to differentiate between these pale, wriggling furballs, as the breed does not generally have distinctive markings. However, even at this stage there are things to look out for.

The most obvious question you will have asked yourself is whether you wish to have a boy or a girl. If you are planning to show or breed from your dog, there will be very different expectations placed upon it, compared to whether you are simply looking for a best friend. If the Golden Retriever breed is really at the top end of the size that your home can accommodate, you may wish to select a female, as these are generally smaller than males as adults. Female dogs may also be less boisterous. If you do not intend to breed from her, however, you will need to consider having her spayed after her first season. This will also eliminate the mess of the 6-monthly season and protect her from pyometra. If you prefer a male dog, you should be prepared to train him out of instincts such as scent marking in the home should this arise, and consider getting him castrated if you do not intend to breed and do not want him chasing after receptive female dogs in the park.

The color of the litter will generally be lighter than their adult coats; however, for an indicator of their adult color you should look at the ears. These may look darker in the puppy and show the shade that the rest of his coat will reach as an adult.

You should be sure that the puppy that catches your eye is clean and does not smell. His coat should feel plush and silky with no scabs or fleas. Check his eyes and ears for discharge and feel his tummy. It should be plump but not hard. If it is distended it may indicate a worm problem.

If you are intending to show your dog, you will be looking for a puppy that shows promise of matching the breed standard, with no unusual markings. This is discussed further in Chapter 15. And if you are looking for a working dog you will want to pick out the highest energy candidate. However, if you are looking for a companion dog, you should just trust for a connection. It is one of those things you can't really qualify—you just know that this particular puppy is destined to be a part of your life.

Considerations of a Rescue Dog

"Regarding rescue dogs; it's important to understand the majority of these dogs are not bred by responsible breeders, often they can come with medical and or temperament issues. That doesn't mean they can't be good pets, but it does mean they can require more diligence with respect to care and training."

Gina Carr
Brier Golden Retrievers

If you have decided on a rescue dog, and have been fortunate enough to find one that you connect with in need of a good home, the first thing you can expect is to be home checked. This isn't as intimidating as it sounds, as the representative of the shelter that visits your home is not looking for dust above the door frames; he or she is simply checking that you live where you say you do, your tenancy agreement if you rent your home allows dogs, your home and garden are secure and free of dangerous objects, that your accommodation is suitable for a large breed dog, and that everyone in the family has thought about the implications of dog ownership and has a basic understanding of what it entails.

If you have owned dogs before, even Golden Retrievers, you should not feel patronized by a home check, as it simply indicates that the rescue is taking its duty of care seriously, and does not wish to place a dog in a situation where it may be returned to the shelter when things do not work out. Having said that, one positive aspect of adopting a rescue dog is that if the unforeseen should happen, the rescue offers full backup, and will take the dog back and find it another home. In fact, this is usually a condition that you sign up to in adopting from a shelter. You do not own the dog and do not have the right to rehome it yourself without the permission of the original rescue organization, who have committed to that dog for the rest of its life to ensure that it is never again let down by humans, and will always have the chance of loving and responsible ownership.

Before the home check, do make sure that you have made any necessary modifications to your yard boundary to ensure a large dog cannot escape. Also, if you rent your home, be sure to have your rental agreement on hand. Failure to do either of these will mean that the home checker will need to return, which will delay the adoption and you could even lose the dog you may have reserved.

If you already have dogs, you may need to participate in a "Meet and Greet" prior to the adoption, to check that your dogs are likely to get along. This is usually on neutral territory, as the new dog would be at a disadvantage in this assessment if it should take place in the home of your existing dog.

Your rescue dog may need special consideration when you bring him or her home. He may feel insecure initially in his new environment and this may manifest itself in behavioral issues that are simply a part of the transitioning process. If you have another dog, they may

Photo Courtesy of Travis Brady

even fight, and you may be ready to give up on the newcomer. But with patience and common sense, these initial teething problems should be overcome. A good rescue organization will always be there to support you, as it is in everyone's interest, not least the dog's, for the arrangement to be a success. If problems persist, a behaviorist may be brought in to see where things could be done better. This does not mean you have failed, but is a pragmatic step to turn things around. The rescue organization may arrange and even pay for professional help should it be required.

Most adoptions, however, are trouble-free, and your new dog will soon be showering you with his appreciation for the new life you have given him. Golden Retrievers are generally a laid-back and adaptable breed, and in no time, it will seem as if he has always been a part of your family.

CHAPTER 5
Preparations for a New Dog

Preparing Your Home

"Do the 'baby crawl' around your house! Just like parents baby proofing their house, you have to puppy proof yours! If you can see it, climb, bite it, or get to it and it's less than a foot off the ground, then so can your puppy!"

Marnie J Harrell
Shadymist Kennel

Whether you are ready to welcome an eight-week-old puppy into your home, or an older dog from a shelter, the weeks leading up to this exciting day should be used to make sure your home is ready for the new arrival.

If you already have a dog or dogs, you may already feel perfectly prepared. There will, however, still be a few things to consider. When securing your yard, you need to consider the size and life-stage of the dog you will be welcoming. If you will be bringing a puppy home, your yard may not necessarily be secure even if you have a dog already. Puppies, obviously, are small, and may wriggle underneath your fence or through small holes that would not present an escape route to your older dog. They also do not yet have any sense of territory, and their natural curiosity will make them more inclined to break out. This also applies to an older dog from a rescue. He does not yet know where he belongs and may seek to return to the place he last knew. So, with an older dog, be sure your yard fence is sufficiently high to stop him leaping over. Six feet is recommended. If your existing fence is not that high, use the weeks before your dog arrives to replace it or add trellis or chain-link fencing. Also remember that dogs will dig, so be sure that the fence goes right down to the ground. If your new dog turns out to be a determined digger, you may have to sink the fence into the ground, or set paving stones around the perimeter of your yard.

Photo Courtesy of
Troy Folsom

A Golden Retriever is a pedigree dog, and as such is a target for thieves. Be sure to place two bolts, top and bottom, on the inside of your yard gate if it does not already have them. A lock is even better. While these measures will not stop a determined thief if your dog is left unattended in the yard, it will prevent an opportunist theft.

Your dog will be using your yard for his toileting and whether you have children or not, clearing up the mess daily is very important for the health of yourself and your family. Think of where to dispose of it, and whether you may wish to divide your yard so that your children may play in a section to which the dog never has access. You may also wish to fence off areas such as a pool or pond as your Golden Retriever will be drawn magnetically to any water. Also, be sure to remove any potentially dangerous items and repair any broken glass in a greenhouse, for example.

Photo Courtesy of Brandon Short

If you are a keen gardener, check that the plants in your yard are not poisonous to dogs, and if so, consider removing them, or replanting in an area to which the dog will not have access. Also, if you use slug pellets or rat bait you will need to remove these and look into more natural methods of pest control.

Inside the home, think about the areas of the house to which your new dog will have access, and where your new dog will sleep. Some owners prefer that their dogs do not go upstairs, in which case you may wish to install a stair gate while your dog learns the boundaries. Stair gates can also section off certain rooms, as you may wish to keep your living room free of dog hair, since Golden Retrievers are such profuse shedders. It is always best to restrict your dog's access from the outset so that he never misses what he has never had, rather than decide later on that you would prefer not to share your bed with a dog.

Chapter 4 discussed how puppies will chew everything. It is in their nature and soothes the pain of teething, as well as providing comfort and alleviating boredom. Therefore, now is the time to remove every movable item that you do not want destroyed, and if you have any expensive items of furniture in the rooms to which your dog will have access, you might consider putting them into storage for a while and refurnishing with cheap or second-hand items. The puppy stage does not last forever, and your dog should not be punished while he is still being taught what he may and may not chew.

50

Your new dog will also inevitably have accidents indoors while he is being housebroken. If you have hard floors, these will be easy enough to deal with, but if you have carpets and wish to keep them, you may consider investing in a carpet shampooer so you can calmly and promptly deal with any mess on the carpet. This is not only a hygiene issue, but a dog will return to areas that smell of his own urine, so it is worth being prepared.

HELPFUL TIP
Picking a Golden Retriever

There are two main breeding lines for Golden Retrievers. Goldens bred primarily for the show ring tend to be fluffier and lighter in color. Anecdotally, they tend to have more health and behavioral problems. Golden Retrievers bred from working lines tend to have redder, less dense coats and tend to have more energy and more stable personalities.

If you have decided to crate-train your dog, think about where to position the crate. This should be somewhere out of drafts and somewhere the dog will feel comfortable. If you will be allowing him in the living room, then a cozy corner where he can feel a part of the family in his own safe space is ideal. If he is to be more restricted, then choose a warm but not too hot part of the kitchen, where he can watch everything going on but will not be too tortured by the smell of cooking bacon. Or a spot in the hallway away from drafts, as dogs often like to settle near the front door. You can put a blanket over the crate to create more of a den for your dog, and cover the front at night so he has some cues about when to settle.

The next thing to consider is how you wish to travel your dog, and for most people, this will be in the car. Chapter 7 deals with all aspects of traveling your dog, and when you have made the decision whether to use a crate, a dog guard, or a harness, you will need to get your chosen accessory fitted in advance of the day when you pick your new dog up. Put some towels and wipes in the car too, in case your dog turns out to be car sick, or in the case of a puppy, to have an accident on the way home. Also, if you have a longer journey to make, be sure to have a lead and collar or harness, a bowl, and a bottle of water so you can stop on the way to give your dog a drink and a comfort break.

If you invest time in the weeks before your new dog's arrival in preparing your home, it will provide a smooth transition for the dog, and any potential stresses from bringing an animal into a human living space will be foreseen and minimized.

Shopping List

Photo Courtesy of
Julie & Holly Simmons
PrairieWyn Golden Retrievers

It can be fun shopping for a new dog, but when you step into the pet store, the array of accessories can be quite overwhelming! So, what do you actually need for your new dog, and specifically for a Golden Retriever?

Crates will also be discussed in Chapter 7, and whether or not you decide to crate-train your dog, it is still useful to have a crate. This can provide an optional den for your dog in the house, it can be used for travel, for separating your dog in certain situations, to protect your home during short absences, and for hospitalization, for example if your dog needs to rest an injury. You can buy wire or fabric crates, either of which pack down for storage or travel. Wire crates also come with covers, but you can use any blanket or towel for the same purpose.

An adult Golden Retriever will require an extra-large crate, which may in any case be too large for your car, but to purchase a crate of this size for a puppy may leave him feeling insecure. So, a medium-size crate that you can use in the car and that will see him through his first nine months is a good start.

The item that is the most fun to choose is your dog's bed. Be aware that your dog may destroy his bed in the early stages, so it may be best to choose a more budget bed as long as the cover looks durable. You may prefer a plastic bed, as these are resilient to chewing and you can make them comfortable with old blankets or towels which are easily washed. If you are buying a puppy, you may be thinking ahead to his fully grown size, but in reality, he will probably have destroyed his bed by the time he reaches maturity, so he may feel more secure in a bed that is not much bigger than his present requirement. Once he has lost his sharp puppy teeth and learned about inappropriate chewing, he may graduate to that expensive, luxurious bed in an extra-large Golden Retriever size!

When you pick up your dog, chances are, he will not already have his own collar and leash, so this is something you will need to pick out. Choose a collar with a wide range of adjustment if you do not already have your dog to know his size. However, do not pick out a check chain;

this is too harsh for your puppy. You will also need a short clip-on leash. At this stage, you will not want a flexi-leash. These leashes are popular but controversial as they can fail to lock, or cause entanglements, and they do not encourage proper training. They have their uses for certain small adult dogs with poor recall, but your Golden Retriever is intelligent enough to learn not to need a flexi-leash, and in any case, his size, strength, and exuberance are not suited to running to the end of a long leash.

A harness is always a good idea because it is more secure than a collar and leash. A dog may back out of its collar, and if the leash is attached to the collar it can cause strain on the delicate bones of the neck. A harness diverts and spreads that strain across the chest area, which is better equipped to deal with it. When training your dog, you will use a collar and leash, but when taking him out into insecure environments, especially near roads, a harness is recommended. You will need a harness appropriate to his current size. Although there is a fair range of adjustability in a harness, you can expect to have to buy larger sizes as your Golden Retriever grows. With a trained adult dog, you will probably find you no longer need a harness for your Golden as they have excellent recall and are generally exercised off-leash.

Your new dog will need at least one food bowl and a separate bowl for water which should be available at all times. These do not necessarily have to come from the pet store; any heavy bowl in the kitchen will do the job.

If you are buying food for your new dog, be sure to have checked what food he is already on, as any change should take place very gradually. The breeder may send you home with some of your dog's current food. If you wish to change him onto something else, wait a few weeks while he settles in, and only then should you mix a little of the new food with his current food, gradually increasing the ratio over a period of a few weeks. This will guard against any tummy upsets from a sudden change of diet.

Although it's fun to shop for a new dog, the cost may seem daunting, but there are ways to keep this to a minimum. For a start, not everything you buy needs to be new. As long as you wash secondhand items thoroughly, you may find the things on your shopping list at yard sales, online auction sites, classified ads, or from friends and family. As already mentioned, you can also use old towels and blankets. Your dog has no concept of what you have spent on his comfort. As long as it is safe and clean, he will appreciate it whether it comes from a designer store or a yard sale! These preferences are purely your own choice.

Introducing Your New Golden Retriever to Other Dogs

Photo Courtesy of Kristin Stohl-Carlson

If you already have a dog or dogs in your home, bringing a newcomer into the family might not go down quite as well with the resident dogs as the excitement you feel yourself. But there is a right and a wrong way of approaching this.

If you are adopting a dog from a shelter, he may have already met your existing dog at a "Meet and Greet," but as this will probably have been on neutral territory, the interaction between the dogs will possibly have been more accepting than when your new dog enters the home environment of a resident dog.

If your new dog and the resident dog have already had a chance to get to know each other on neutral ground, such as a dog walk, this is a good start. However, in most cases, the first time they will meet is when you bring your new dog home.

To begin with, it is a bad idea to open the front door with your new dog and let them meet for the first time inside the home on the resident dog's territory, even if your resident dog is used to visiting dogs. To get off to the best start, you should take your resident dog into the yard and distract him for a while, while your partner or a helper settles the new dog inside the home. Once the new dog has calmed down to a reasonable level, allow your resident dog inside to meet his new friend. Try to avoid the temptation to intervene too much in their initial contact with each other and give them plenty of space. The atmosphere may seem charged, and there may even be some scrapping; this is all part of sorting out the new dynamics. You should be there to monitor the situation and separate the dogs if necessary, but a heavy-handed approach will not help the dogs establish their own relationship, so you should only step in if you have to. Letting the dogs into the securely enclosed yard together is a good next step, as they will be better inclined to get along in a less confined space.

If your resident dog is an adult and you have brought a puppy into the home, you may expect your existing dog to teach the little upstart some manners in the early weeks, so you should not be too alarmed if your older dog reacts negatively to the puppy's exuberant invasion of his personal space. Using a crate for the puppy can give your older dog some time out. They will sort things out between them in time, and it can be an advantage to the puppy to receive an education from your adult dog as well as the training and socialization with which you will be providing him.

Introducing your new Golden Retriever to other dogs outside the home is a vital stage in his life if he is a puppy, as the first 14 weeks of his life are critical for socialization. If during this vital period he has not been exposed to many different environments and to other humans and dogs, it may cause him to be fearful throughout his life. So, if you get your puppy at eight weeks of age, you have six important weeks to fill with as many social opportunities as possible. As your puppy will not yet have full immunity from his first course of vaccinations, he will not yet be able to go out into public places where unvaccinated dogs will have been; however, vets often run puppy classes that are open to dogs as soon as they have had the first of their initial vaccinations, so you should inquire about these with your veterinarian. Your puppy may of course meet your friends' dogs as long as they are fully vaccinated.

If you have taken on a rescue dog, he will naturally have had a lot of exposure to other dogs, but if he has had bad experiences in the past, there may be some psychological barriers to be overcome. Your rescue dog may even have a phobia of certain breeds if he has been attacked in the past. Although most rescue dogs do not come with this sort of baggage, if it is something that arises, you may need to carefully re-socialize your dog by setting up good experiences for him, allowing him play dates with selected docile dogs amongst your circle of acquaintances. Golden Retrievers are especially attracted to their own breed, so if you know someone with a calm and gentle Golden, this will be an asset in helping your dog overcome their fear. When you are out in public in uncontrolled situations, however, you will always need to stay one step ahead in anticipating negative situations and averting them without any sense of panic that may transmit to your dog. Learn to read the body language of other dogs, and always walk your dog away if things are looking like they may turn ugly. You need to build up good experiences for your fearful dog and he will learn to trust you and grow in confidence. It is your responsibility, however, to muzzle your dog in public if he is the potential aggressor.

Introducing Your New Golden Retriever to Children

If you are adopting a Golden Retriever from a rescue, the organization will have assessed the dog first and will not place a fearful dog with a family that has children because of the risk that the dog will bite, and will also be very stressed. Consequently, if you have children and a reputable rescue has allowed you to adopt a Golden Retriever from them, the dog will have been child-tested, and your work is partly done. At least from the dog's perspective. The other part is in educating your children.

In the weeks leading up to the arrival of your new dog, whether it is a puppy or an adult Golden Retriever, you should take your children to meet as many child-friendly dogs as possible, especially larger dogs, as your Golden Retriever will grow rapidly if he is not already an adult, and your children need to know how to respect a dog.

Show your child how to approach the dog gently, offering a closed fist for the dog to sniff. Then allow your child to stroke the back of the dog's neck. Teach them never to poke the dog or pull its ears, tail, or coat, and never to shout at the dog, or touch it when it is eating, chewing, or sleeping. Make sure the child knows that the way to play with a dog

Photo Courtesy of Curtis McCollough

is with safe toys, as rough play encourages aggression. If your child is older, show them how they can be involved in the dog's daily care, feeding, grooming, playing, walking, and training the dog with you.

The dynamic between a child and a dog is not the same as with an adult. A dog may attempt to dominate a child, in establishing its place in the pecking order between the adult carer and the subordinate child. This can lead to the dog snapping or snarling at the child, which is a major barrier to a happy relationship. Fortunately, the Golden Retriever is renowned as a perfect family dog, as well as being very trainable and eager to please, so teaching the dog its place in the pack should not be too difficult. However, if problems persist, it is worth consulting a behaviorist to see if anything could be done better before the undesirable behavior becomes too entrenched.

It is worth bearing in mind in a family situation with young children, that allowing the dog to sleep in the bedroom with its adult humans, or even on their bed, may encourage delusions of superiority in the dog. Therefore, from the outset, if there are young children in the home, the dog should be trained to sleep downstairs. Involving the children in training and feeding the dog also helps to establish their position of authority above the dog so they are less likely to be challenged.

For a child, growing up with a dog is a unique education. It teaches care and respect, gentleness, and responsibility. It encourages physical exercise, and studies even show that exposure to dogs decreases allergies and asthma in young children . It also teaches a child how to cope with the heartbreak of bereavement, a tough but necessary lesson for later life. The choice of a Golden Retriever not only provides your child with a best friend, but will shape his or her character and set them up for the future.

CHAPTER 6
Training

"Goldens are very easy to train. One of their best attributes is how much they love to please people and they want to do the things their owner's request."

Angel Martin
Goldensglen Goldens

As we have said before in this book, your Golden Retriever is an intelligent dog. The characteristic that is officially used to describe him by the breed standard is "biddable," which means eager to please. So, all he is waiting for are your instructions! There is a reason why Golden Retrievers are used as assistance dogs and in search and rescue, and that is because they are so trainable. From the very beginning you can set high expectations for your dog. Even if you are not aiming for a TV talent show, a well-trained dog will fit in with your life so much more easily, and in turn your dog will be happier. With a large dog like a Golden Retriever, training is the key to a harmonious family relationship.

The key to teaching your dog to obey your rules lies in associative training. This is a principle that creates connections in your dog's brain, as evidenced in the case of Pavlov's dog. In the early 1900s, an experimental scientist named Ivan Pavlov, who was investigating canine digestive function, noticed that his subjects would salivate when presented with food. He then introduced a specific sound at meal times, and found that even when food was not present, the dogs would still salivate at the sound, demonstrating that a dog can form associations in the brain, a process termed "classical conditioning."

Remember the key to successful training is to get your dog to focus his attention on you. Take a hint from Pavlov's dog that food is an excellent motivator. Golden Retrievers are very food oriented so training with a treat in your hand will produce rapid results. You can just use a portion of his regular kibble for training; otherwise, you can use small training treats or tiny pieces of baked liver so you don't build too many extra calories into your dog's daily ration. Whatever your choice, you should adjust his meal portions accordingly. Praise also means a lot to your dog, and as you progress, you can reduce the treats and just reward him with a lot of fuss for doing the right thing.

Photo Courtesy of
Dylan Starer

Toilet Training

Photo Courtesy of
Amanda and Erik Allworth
Photographer – Kristina Noel Photography

For the purposes of this section, we will assume you are bringing home a puppy. However, if you have adopted or purchased an adult dog that perhaps has lived in kennels or not been properly trained, the method of toilet training, or housebreaking, is broadly the same. The difference between a puppy and an adult dog is that the puppy does not yet have full control of his bladder and bowels. Therefore, however much he may want to please you when he realizes outside is the place to toilet, if he is not being taken outside regularly enough, he may involuntarily mess inside the house. On the other hand, an adult dog in most cases has the physical control, but his habits are more deeply ingrained. In both cases, patience is the key, and success should follow sooner or later.

There are different strategies to housebreaking your dog. The first is active supervision, always being ready to take your dog outside; the second is to restrict your dog's access to the home in the early stages by closing doors, using play pens, or installing stair gates; and the third is crate-training. However, all these approaches require a scheduled routine of toilet breaks, which should include extra breaks after eating, drinking, playing, or awaking from a nap.

The basic principle of toilet training is for your dog to learn by association the appropriate place to urinate or defecate. In this regard he is guided by two things: scent and texture. Using puppy pads inside the home can be counterproductive, because the dog will associate soft surfaces such as furnishings and clothes with acceptable places to toilet. From the outset, he needs to recognize the texture of grass under his paws to encourage him to toilet outside. Therefore, it is vital to take him out very regularly in the early stages, so that he has ample opportunity to toilet in the appropriate place. Initially he will not know what is expected of him, so patience is needed to wait out that moment when he starts to toilet. At this moment, and not before, you may use your command word (e.g., "Busy") so that he associates the word with the action. You may use this command once it is learned to promote the action, but not until he understands it, otherwise you will be fruitlessly using the command in connection with an action he is not doing, and the association will be lost.

After your dog has toileted in the correct place you should make a big fuss over him and give him a treat. If you are clicker-training (which is a method of reinforcing associative training) then click and reward immediately after your dog has completed his business. Don't distract him with praise and reward while he is actually in the process as he may not finish the job.

Once your dog has been toileting appropriately outdoors for a while, the task will become easier, as he will have set up areas where he recognizes his scent. You may also find he is naturally inclined to urinate outdoors to cover the scents of any passing wildlife or neighborhood cats that may have visited your yard.

While your dog's sensitive nose can work to your advantage in this way, it can be a problem if he has toileted indoors and the soiled area has not been cleaned adequately, as he will return to this area and toilet again. It is important to use an enzymatic cleaner to break down the urea in the soiled area, and not to use any cleaner containing ammonia, which smells like urine to a dog. You may then go over the area thoroughly with a carpet shampooer if you have one, to prevent staining.

One of the worst mistakes an owner can make in housebreaking their dog is to use harsh punishment. Your Golden Retriever learns by association, so if he is punished when he is caught toileting indoors, he associates the punishment with doing the action in the presence of his human, not with doing it in an inappropriate place. He then may become a "stealth toileter," sneaking away to toilet indoors privately. The right action to take when catching your dog in the act is to say "No" firmly and whisk him outside where you can give him a reassuring pat. If you find the evidence but have missed the action, the moment is lost for stern words, so you should just clean up and resume positive toilet training at the next opportunity.

Patient and consistent training with plenty of toileting opportunities should soon result in a housebroken dog, but be sure not to stop toilet training your dog when you think he has "got it." The habit needs to become deeply ingrained, so you should continue with positive reinforcement long after seeing results. If at any stage, however, your previously housebroken dog should start to regress and toilet in the house again, it is worth seeing your veterinarian, as this can be symptomatic of illness or infection. Alternatively, if it is a psychological issue, a behaviorist may help you work through an unexplained change in your dog's habits. For a dog as intelligent as a Golden Retriever to regress is an unusual step, so it should always be taken seriously. A formerly housebroken dog knows the rules and will be as troubled about displeasing you as you are to find him soiling the home again.

How to Teach Sit

HELPFUL TIP
Exercise is Key

Since Golden Retrievers were born to be working dogs, they have a lot of energy and need tons of exercise. If your Golden is having a hard time focusing during training sessions, try taking him for a long walk or a run first to burn off excess energy.

The first command you will teach your dog is to "Sit." Not only is this a vital command for your dog's own safety in certain situations, but it is a simple first step in the journey of communication with your dog.

Get your dog's attention fully on you. This will not be a problem with a Golden Retriever, as the only thing he loves more than his human is his human with food in their hand. Now with a smooth motion, guide the dog into the sit position by moving your hand with the treat up and over his head. His hindquarters will instinctively lower. Only when his bottom is fully on the floor do you give your dog the treat and praise him.

(If you are clicker-training your dog, you will click as well as treat at each point he does the right thing. Clickers are an optional extra associative reinforcement that the action is correct.)

At this stage, you are not using any command word. Only once the action is firmly in place after several repetitions should you use the word "Sit" as you do the hand motion, as you can reliably predict that it will result in a sit. This way the word becomes associated with the action in your dog's brain.

With further repetitions, you can wean your dog off the hand signal by making the gesture smaller, until you are using no hand signal or body language at all, but just the word to produce a sit in your dog. Your timing is very important in rewarding the correct behavior with a treat and praise.

The next step is to wean the dog off the treat altogether, since in practice you will not have a treat on hand every time you want your dog to sit; neither would this be good for his waistline. So, as you continue the command, do not treat on every repetition. You can still praise your dog, but just produce the treat on intermittent repetitions.

You do not have to reach all these stages in one training session. Keep sessions short for your dog and end on a positive note. Build training into his daily routine so it soon becomes second nature, and it will not be a chore for either of you!

How to Teach Stay

Although the command "Stay" can be taught along with the word, another method is the "Silent Stay." This assumes that after you have placed your dog in the sit, you wish him to stay in that position until he is released from it by you. "Stay" therefore does not need a word, but your dog may be released by a word such as "Free."

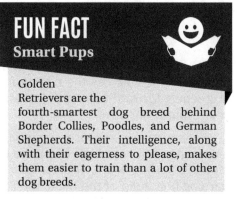

FUN FACT
Smart Pups

Golden Retrievers are the fourth-smartest dog breed behind Border Collies, Poodles, and German Shepherds. Their intelligence, along with their eagerness to please, makes them easier to train than a lot of other dog breeds.

To teach this method, place your dog in the sit, and keep his attention by telling him he is a good boy. Then when he is sitting attentively, you may lead him away from the sit with a treat in your hand. As he gets up, use the word "Free."

In the first stages, you will need to keep the time in sit very short, before your dog loses attention and gets up of his own accord. You need to stay in control of his actions. He will soon learn he gets a treat by staying until you release him. Increase the time in silent stay as you progress, including walking away from him before you release him from the position.

If you wish to use the word "Stay" while he is staying to reinforce the point, there is nothing wrong with this, but you should still use the word "Free" to release your dog from this position.

How to Teach Lie Down

Photo Courtesy of Claire Moody

It is easiest to start teaching the lie down command from a sit position, so you should ask your dog to sit, and reward him to focus his attention on you.

Kneel in front of your dog, so that you have good eye contact, and bring a treat to his nose, then lower the treat in your closed hand to the floor between his legs and close to his body. Your dog should instinctively lower his front legs, but you should not reward him until both elbows are firmly on the floor. His hind quarters should also go down, but if they do not, you should not push them, which creates resistance, rather you should use your other arm like a limbo pole. Place it across the dog's back, and move the treat forward, so in creeping forward toward the treat, the dog has to lower his back beneath your other arm.

Repeating this exercise many times in succession should lead to a more automatic response, but in the unlikely event that your Golden Retriever is slow to learn, you can teach the command incrementally, rewarding first a dip of the head, then a lowering of the elbows, until you have achieved the full lie down position.

Once your dog sits nicely with you kneeling beside him, raise your body to a crouch and then a stand, which will add to the challenge, as you will not be bringing the treat all the way to the floor for his nose to follow.

As with "Sit," you should not use the command "Lie Down" until your dog is reliably being guided into the correct position with the treat. The next step is to wean him off the treat so that he acts consistently on the word alone. As with "Sit," do not reward on every repetition, but vary the times he gets a treat or just some fuss.

Adding the silent stay to the lie down command is the next step, so that you have a dog that will lie down and stay down, which can be extremely useful when you have visitors. Just as with stay, you should release your dog from the position with the word "Free." Initially, release him after only a few seconds, building up the time he remains in the lie down position. But remember to release him at the end of the training session, or your obedient dog may be too afraid to get up and will remain forgotten in the lying down position!

How to Teach Walk On the Leash

Your Golden Retriever puppy is going to grow into a large, strong dog, so teaching him to walk nicely on a loose leash is vitally important from the outset. The initial difficulty is that puppies are naturally exuberant, and will be more inclined to jump around and bite the leash than be led nicely by it at their owner's heels. Achieving this objective is going to take time and patience.

You need to have realistic expectations about walks when leash training your dog. This is because you will not be going consistently in one direction or at one speed. You will also have to work to keep your dog's full attention by being an exciting person to be around, and more interesting than his surroundings. To your dog, the leash is an impediment to going where he wants, and he will instinctively pull. He needs to disassociate pulling with getting where he wants, and associate going forward with the feeling of a loose leash. This means every time he pulls, you will stop. Put him in the sit so that you can regain a loose leash, then proceed. Your walk is going to be a continual sequence of stopping and starting in the early stages, and you should also keep changing direction to keep your dog interested. Eventually, he will realize there is a lot more walking and a lot less stopping and sitting when the leash connection is loose, and he will deduce that the right place to be is by your side. Have your training treats on hand so you can reinforce his correct behavior when he is walking nicely as you would wish.

If you are attending puppy classes, you may find your Golden Retriever puppy learns very quickly in class and walks beautifully on the leash. However, once you are outside on a walk, he is a hooligan. This is hardly surprising, as there are so many more distractions in the big outdoors. Your challenge is in working that bit harder to maintain his attention outside, as you already know he can do it in a different environment. It may feel frustrating when you just want a nice stroll in the park with your dog, but this time will come. The early months are for training which is a different experience altogether, but a totally worthwhile investment for the years to come.

How to Teach Walk Off the Leash

Your Golden Retriever was bred for working in the field and as a consequence, it is natural for him to romp off leash and expend much more of his boundless energy in doing so than he would if trotting at your heels for the same amount of time. The initial problem in reaching this stage of confidence is getting him to come back.

Just as you invest your time and energy in teaching commands like sit, lie down, and stay to your dog, you are inadvertently also teaching recall, because you are establishing a bond between yourself and your dog, and exerting your position as master and pack leader as well as teaching him his name. Your Golden Retriever wants to please you and is a very devoted breed, so naturally he wants to come back to you. The problem may be that he wishes to do this in his own time.

As with your previous training, you should carry treats in your pocket when teaching recall. That rabbit scent will need to be very distracting to a Golden Retriever to divert him from a food treat. Some Goldens also find a ball very motivating in staying focused on their owners off the leash. You do need to give your dog permission to go away from you, however, otherwise being off leash will not have the result that your dog can run freely, for the good of his mind and body. So, while calling him back regularly and treating him for his prompt attention, you should release him again with the "Free" command. The command "Come" is preferred for recall, as it is more associative with the action than simply calling the dog's name.

Begin recall training in a safe enclosed space before venturing into open countryside. A flexi-leash will not be helpful to you in teaching your dog to walk off leash, as your dog will still sense the contact, and it does not provide sufficient range. A training line, however, may be useful if you do not have an enclosed space and your dog might run off. These are extremely long, and should be lightweight. They should be attached to a harness so that if your dog runs to the end of it, he does not suddenly get a harsh jerk to the neck. The dog will have very little sensation of being attached to a leash, but you have the security of being able to bring him back from a far distance if all else fails. Training leashes should not be used near other people or dogs, however, as they risk entanglement.

One thing worth noting is that your Golden may soon learn recall; it is in their nature, and he may return at your command very reliably. However, at adolescence, many dogs regress temporarily. In a Golden Retriever this is around 8-18 months of age. This can be a challenging period as your dog becomes driven by his own instincts, and while it may

Photo Courtesy of
Jamie Smith

affect all his training, recall can be the most alarming thing to lose because of the danger of losing your dog. If you notice your dog becoming more disobedient about coming back from the age of 8 months, don't panic as this is only a phase. However, you may wish to consider walking him in more confined spaces for a while, such as the park rather than open countryside, and be sure that he is wearing a collar and tag in case he should stray. You may even wish to go back to the training leash and to treats in your pocket, but don't be discouraged, as after this brief period your dog will be ready to settle into adult life, with all his early training magically back in place.

Agility and Flyball

Golden Retrievers are excellently suited to Agility because they are so intelligent and athletic. If you have a high-energy dog, Agility can help a great deal in managing his hyperactivity, and provide a fun pastime that will keep you both in good shape.

Young puppies cannot participate in Agility because of the risk of damaging growing bones and growth plates. However, those early months may profitably be used in obedience training so that when your dog can start with the basics of Agility at twelve months, his focus is on his master and he understands about following commands and the principles of reward training.

Agility involves taking your dog around an obstacle course against the clock, and is graded so that initially your dog will only be jumping very low poles. At this stage he will also learn the other elements of the course, such as the tunnel, hoops, the A-frame, the walkway, the see-saw, and the weaves. As his bones and joints reach maturity, the course becomes more demanding. Most Golden Retrievers will love the challenge and exercise involved in Agility and it will increase your bond. If, however, your dog doesn't seem to be enjoying it and seems stressed by the experience, you may need to accept that his personality is different and look instead for what he really enjoys.

Flyball is another exciting pastime that your Golden Retriever may enjoy, as it involves retrieving a ball from the end of an obstacle course and returning with it, and naturally, retrieving is your dog's greatest skill!

If you are less mobile and would find running an Agility course with your dog problematic, Flyball may be a more attractive option, as for the most part, the dog is going it alone.

As with Agility, your dog needs to be twelve months before starting Flyball to ensure his growth plates are closed, but the initial stages will only involve low jumps. Your dog should have good recall, because he will be sent away down the course to retrieve the ball before returning, but beginners' runs are usually fenced each side.

In the early months before your dog starts Flyball, your obedience training is providing a sure foundation. Fitness and diet are also very important for a dog that is going to take part in high-energy activities such as Agility and Flyball.

Starting out with a Golden Retriever is very exciting because of their innate ability to learn. Training a Golden is very rewarding, and leads to a connection that really shows why dogs are known as man's best friend. As such, the Golden Retriever is the best possible ambassador for its species, and actually, almost human!

CHAPTER 7
Traveling

"Goldens make wonderful travel companions. They have a sense of adventure and are extroverts. Goldens want to come along with their owners everywhere they go, and center their lives around being with their humans."

Jill Simmons
PoeticGold Farm

Preparations for Travel

Most owners will have multiple situations, during the lifetime of their dog, when they will need to travel with him. This might be simply a short distance, for example to the vet or to a regular walking place, or it could be a long journey, even possibly internationally.

You have more options than just traveling in a car with your dog. Dogs are often allowed on public transport as well, even trains and aircraft. There will be very different preparation needs depending on the type and length of travel.

If you are going on a long trip, it is a good idea to prepare for travel with a trip to your veterinarian first. This is vital because you should not travel long distances with your dog if he is not well. A general check-up will make sure his health is in top form. This is also an excellent opportunity to check that all vaccinations are up to date. If not, your dog can have a booster vaccination at this time. You can pick up flea and worming prevention for the time you are traveling at this appointment too, so these do not lapse, and any ongoing chronic medications to make sure there isn't a break in administration if you otherwise would have run out while you are away. If you are traveling internationally, most countries will require the rabies vaccination to be up to date, and may even require a blood test to prove the vaccine has been effective. In addition, for some destinations, export paperwork may need to be completed, as well as a passport and vaccine records. These can all be signed by your veterinarian at this time. It is important to remember that it is your responsibili-

Photo Courtesy of David A Ring

ty that your veterinarian has signed all the relevant paperwork for your dog, so make sure you do your reading up on what is required for the location you are traveling to.

If your dog needs to see a veterinarian while you are away, which hopefully will not be the case, you must find the most local one who can see him. Spend some time looking up the local veterinarians in the area you will be in, and key into your phone the contact details in case of an emergency. Also ensure the contact details of your regular veterinarian are close at hand, as they might want to contact them to share medical details.

When you are away, if your dog were to escape, it is not in its local area and therefore is unlikely to return home. Therefore, it is a responsible thing to do to ensure your dog has identification on him. A microchip is the best, as this is a permanent form of identification. Ensure your contact details are up to date with the microchip company, though, as a microchip which is registered to an old address or cell number is useless. Another form of identification used is a collar with an ID tag on it. The tag should have the number to contact on it, as well as an address. Some people prefer not to have the dog's name on the tag, as otherwise someone with poor intentions will be able to call the dog. While you are away, you can put on a temporary tag with the location you are staying at if you wish, although this is not as necessary as the tag with the home details on.

Traveling in a Car

Photo Courtesy of Kylee Cohoon

It is surprising how well many dogs will tolerate driving in a car, but if your dog is one that doesn't tolerate it, then there might be some simple solutions. You can practice traveling with your dog before the journey, in the case that he is nervous, by initially allowing him to sit in the car on the driveway. He can have his dinner in there or play with you for a while, so that he knows it's an enjoyable place to be. Before a long journey in a car, you can practice driving some short journeys to get your dog used to the motion of the car.

If your dog doesn't get anxious in the car, but actually he gets sick or drools, this might be a sign of nausea. Like humans, dogs can get travel sick. If you are traveling just a short journey, you can travel your dog on an empty stomach, which will aid the nausea. However, if you have a long journey to go on, then there are excellent travel sickness pills which you can request from your veterinarian and give to your dog 30 minutes before the journey.

When you travel with your dog in the car, there are several options to secure your dog. There is no right or wrong way, but some owners will prefer one over another. The first option is to travel your dog in a crate in the hatch of the car. If you have crate-trained your dog from a young age, this is an excellent option as the crate will be seen by your dog as a safe haven, and therefore it will help reduce any anxiety in the car. The crate should be large enough for your dog to stand up, turn around, and lie down without touching the sides, which means it must be fairly large for a Golden Retriever. It should be made of wire or a strong material, with breathable sides such as mesh. It must be placed in the trunk of the car so that there is airflow through it, to ensure it does not get too hot or stuffy inside for your dog. There should also be no sharp projections inside which your dog can hurt themselves on.

If you don't like the idea of a crate, you could put your dog in the hatch of the car without one. This way your dog is a little freer to move around and look out of the windows. Your dog might see this as an opportunity to jump over the back of the seats to join you in the main section of the car though, so if you choose this option, it is worth investing in a dog guard to stop this from happening.

Photo Courtesy of Linda Walkowiak

The safest way for your dog to travel, though, is with a dog harness attached to a seatbelt. These can be purchased from many pet stores and online, and fix onto the seat belts in the back. If you were to be involved in an accident, this ensures that your dog does not come to harm which could have been avoided. It also makes sure they stay in one place and won't try to join you while you are driving, which is very important for safety and may invalidate your insurance. Some people may not like this option, as it will require your dog to take up a seat which could be occupied by a human, and it will also mean the back seats may become covered in hair and drool. However, this last point can be easily overcome by using a cover for the seats when the dog is in the car. Covers can be specially made for dogs which cover the entirety of the back seats.

When you travel with your whole family, including your dog, your children may become bored. While your dog might usually provide excellent entertainment for them, make sure your children do not tease or coax the dog while you are traveling, as your dog does not have the opportunity to move away from them if he wishes to do so. This can make the journey unpleasant for the dog.

Also, ensure that everything you might need is all easily accessible. This includes water and food for your dog, as well as a lead. Your dog should be offered water every 4 hours, and food at least every 12 hours. He will also be appreciative if you allow him to exercise and relieve himself frequently, as sitting in the car for long periods of time can become uncomfortable. If you stop to quickly go to a shop or get fuel, never leave your dog unattended in the car. Dogs can quickly die in cars which do not have open windows or air conditioning.

Traveling by Plane

HELPFUL TIP
Hotel Rules

While more ho-
tels are becoming dog-friendly, many
dog-friendly hotels have size restric-
tions, so be sure to call ahead to make
sure your Golden Retriever will be welcome. Many dog-friendly hotels also
have rules that dogs are not allowed to
be left alone in the rooms. Make sure
you are aware of all the rules regarding your dog and follow them during
the stay, so the hotel doesn't reconsider
their dog policy going forward.

If you are traveling by plane, especially if it is internationally, do your research well, as different airlines and different countries have different requirements. Most airlines require a certificate of health which is no older than 10 days old before travel. This can be provided by your veterinarian. In addition to this, passports, exportation paperwork, and vaccines, especially rabies, must all be completed and up to date.

Most airlines will require the dog to be in a crate, and while some small breeds of dog will be allowed in the cabin, unfortunately your Golden Retriever will almost certainly have to travel in the hold. The exception will be if your dog is a service dog of some type. The airline you are traveling with will be able to provide you with specifications for the crate required. Your dog will not be allowed to travel if it is less than 8 weeks old. Some airlines, however, set their minimum age at 12 weeks.

If the temperature is likely to be below 45 degrees Fahrenheit or above 85 degrees Fahrenheit during departure, arrival, and connections, your dog will not be allowed to travel. Some exceptions may be made if your dog is used to these conditions, but you must present a veterinary certificate explaining this, and then the maximum duration allowed at these temperatures is 4 hours.

Vacation Lodging

Before you book your vacation lodging, contact the company to make sure they allow dogs in their residences. Many vacation locations will not allow dogs. If you are lucky enough to vacation in a place which is dog-friendly, then it is important to be mindful that not everyone at that location might be used to, or even like, dogs. Try to keep your dog quiet, so don't leave him by himself if this is likely to cause him to bark. Also, when you walk him, ensure you pick up anything he has done on the walk. When you arrive at the lodging, ask the receptionist where is best for you to walk your dog, as there may be areas which are off limits.

Try to respect that the accommodation does not belong to you, and after you leave, other guests will arrive. Therefore, do not allow your dog to soil in the room, or destroy furnishings. The room should be able to be returned to a dog-free state with a simple clean.

Leaving Your Dog at Home

If you do not wish to travel with your Golden Retriever, there are many options for where to leave your dog when you are away.

The first option is to ask friends or family to look after your dog. This is often done as a favor rather than as a paid service, so try to make it as easy as possible for your friend or family member. The positive aspect of this is that you personally know the person looking after your dog, and can vouch for their responsibility. You also know what the place is like where your dog is staying. Make sure you leave enough of your dog's food with them, and bring their bed, toys, and lead or harness so that

Photo Courtesy of Heather Dawson

they do not need to provide these things. If your friend or family member has a dog of their own, then make sure you test out the dogs together before leaving your dog. The other dog may not be pleased to have a new dog in his territory, so allow them to meet on neutral ground, such as a walk, or in the yard.

Another option for your Golden Retriever is to book him into a local kennel. Kennels have a reputation for being harsh, but there are actually some exceptionally well-run kennels around and so it is worth doing your research and reading up on reviews before choosing a kennel establishment. In a kennel, dogs will be housed in indoor or outdoor runs, which usually consist of a small area to walk around in, with an area to sleep or rest in at the back. Once or twice a day, they will be let out from this area to either a large communal area or taken on a walk. This allows them to exercise and play with other dogs. Kennels are usually run by very experienced dog handlers; however, your dog will not get one-to-one attention like they would elsewhere. Your dog will require up-to-date vaccinations before being allowed to stay in a kennel establishment, so make sure you have done this and asked your veterinarian to provide you with a signed record before dropping off your dog.

Finally, the most expensive, but probably the best option with regards to security, is to hire a house or dog sitter to come and stay in your house while you are away. This ensures your dog is cared for in their own environment. This is the least uprooting option for your dog. House sitters do not need formal qualifications, so make sure they are professional and have experience before booking them. It might be a good idea to ask them if they would like to come on a dog walk with you or come over to your house so that your dog can get used to them.

Whether you decide to travel with your dog or not, a vacation should be a fun experience for all. So, try not to worry about it and plan plenty in advance. That way both you and your Golden Retriever can enjoy it to the maximum.

CHAPTER 8
Nutrition

Importance of Nutrition

"We give our Goldens wild caught fish oil and eggs, this helps the skin and coat to remain beautiful and soft. Since Goldens are more prone to cancer than many other breeds, it's wise to not skimp when it comes to food and give nutritionally balanced whole food, raw diets if possible. Or make sure cheap fillers such as corn, wheat and soy are not present."

Katie
Grizzly Kennels

Nutrition plays a vital role in your Golden Retriever's day-to-day life, and therefore it is to his benefit that due diligence is paid to ensuring he is on an excellent balanced diet. This will be rewarding for both you and him, as a suitable diet will allow him to be in prime health, full of energy, and feeling great, which in turn will ensure you have a playful, happy Golden Retriever, like they should be.

With so much choice on the market, it can be tricky to decide what to give your dog. Golden Retrievers are adaptable to many foods; however, there are some specific things to look out for when browsing the shelves. They have a luscious long coat, which will benefit greatly from a diet which is rich in omega-3 and omega-6 fatty acids. These will help support the skin in being an effective barrier, as well as allow the coat to be full of vitality. Another thing that omega-3 and omega-6 help is to keep the joints in good working order. As will be discussed in Chapter 12, Golden Retrievers can be prone to joint health issues. Omega fatty acids help keep the joint fluid viscous and well lubricated, as well as decrease inflammation.

If you would like help choosing the most suitable diet for your Golden Retriever, the best person to consult is a dog nutritionist. Many owners, breeders, and even veterinarians will claim that they know the best food for you to give your dog; however, to obtain unbiased, holistic, and professional advice, a dog nutritionist will be your best resource.

Commercial Food

Most pet stores and veterinary clinics will offer a great variety of dog food, which comes in many different types of preparations from many different brands. The choice can be overwhelming, especially to a new owner who has never had a dog before.

When you pick up your new Golden Retriever puppy from the breeder, the best choice of food for your puppy is to in fact carry on with what the breeder has been feeding him. This should be a commercial, nutritionally complete puppy food. The exception to this is if the breeder was feeding the puppy a BARF diet, which will be discussed further in this chapter. Keeping the puppy on the same food will ensure that his stomach does not become upset when everything else is changing in his life. If you wish to change him onto another brand of food, it is best to do this gradually, over the course of a few weeks. The change can be made once he has had a week or two to settle into his new home.

A puppy should always be on a food which states it is for puppies or junior dogs. The reason behind this is that puppies have different nu-

Photo Courtesy of Kellie Blood

tritional and growth requirements than adults. As they are growing, they need significantly more protein to develop muscle strength, more calories per pound of body weight for all the excited energy that they are burning off, and different amounts of calcium and phosphorus than adults, to ensure their bones grow healthy and strong.

As they reach adult size, which is around 9-18 months old, they can be slowly switched onto an adult food. Some owners choose to feed their dog "young adult" or "active dog" food during these younger adult years, and while these are highly beneficial for a young, bouncy Golden Retriever, they are not vital.

Just as younger dogs have the option of special food for their life stage, older dogs also have the option of senior food. Senior food will ensure your elderly dog keeps in top form when his health may be beginning to dwindle, but more will be discussed about senior diets in Chapter 16.

In addition to the choice of life stage food, commercial foods are also offered in both wet and dry preparations. Most owners will have a preference for which they perceive is best; however, there are pros and cons to both, and there is nothing wrong with feeding a mixture.

Wet food is perceived as more palatable than dry food, so if you have one of the rare cases of a picky eating Golden Retriever, he may find this more appetizing. Wet food is much closer to the natural food a dog would eat in the wild and will usually have a meat-protein source as the main ingredient. Most wet foods are over 70% moisture, though, so to feed an entirely wet food diet, your dog may require quite a lot of cans of food per day.

Dry food, however, is much more concentrated in terms of nutrients. A high-quality dry food will only require a small volume to be fed for the dog to receive all the daily nutrients he needs. Unfortunately, dry food can be bulked out with nutritionally void starchy fillers, so when purchasing a dry dog food, it must be of high quality and have a meat component as the main ingredient. Dry dog food is far more beneficial for your dog's teeth, compared to wet food, as dry food will help remove any tartar accumulating on the teeth as the dog crunches through the kibble.

Rest assured, though, if a dog food is on a shelf, it must have met the Association of American Feed Control Officials (AAFCO) standards. These are standards required of all dog food to make sure they contain at least the minimum amount of vitamins, minerals, and nutrients required for a healthy dog. They have two categories—maintenance and growth—therefore, if a dog food has made it to market, it will have passed the standards in one of these categories.

BARF and Homemade Diets

BARF (bones and raw food) diets and homemade diets are becoming very popular within the dog-owning world. It is easy to see why, as these diets allow you to feed natural, non-processed ingredients to your dog on a daily basis. You know exactly what the dog is eating, and have the ability to choose locally sourced, organic, non-GMO food for your dog. Not only this, you have the ability to feed your dog a much more natural diet, closer to what their wolf ancestors would have eaten, rather than processed foods.

However, with these pros come many cons. BARF and homemade diets are extremely difficult to conform to the AAFCO standards, and are usually nutritionally deficient in many minerals. A specialized dog nutritionist can inform you what other minerals you must add to the diet to make it balanced, but very few owners seek this professional help. Mineral deficiencies can lead to ill health, weak bones (especially in growing dogs), stunted growth, and bladder stones. In addition to this, the BARF diet in particular can be extremely dangerous, as bones can get lodged in the intestines, causing life-threatening blockages. Raw meat is also filled with bacteria such as salmonella and E. coli, and while a dog's intestine is relatively strong against small burdens of these bacteria, they will still be found in the feces and saliva of the dog. This can be a major hazard to vulnerable people such as children and the elderly, and since the Golden Retriever is often a family dog, these things need to be taken into consideration and household hygiene is very important.

Pet Food Labels

All pet food labels will have several sections to them which are compulsory to make available to the public. These sections will help you decide if the food is right for your dog and whether the quality is as you would hope.

Guaranteed Analysis

The guaranteed analysis is the percentage of protein, carbohydrates, fat, ash, moisture, and fiber which can be found in the food on an "as fed" basis. Due to this, dry food and wet food cannot be compared directly. There are some simple calculations which can be done to convert the values into a "dry matter" basis which then allows for direct comparison of the foods.

For example, if a wet food is 75% wet, then it means the dry content is 25%. If the protein level is then 5%, this can be converted by dividing by the dry matter percentage: 5/0.25 = 20% protein on a dry matter basis.

Then if a similar dry food, which you wanted to compare, had a moisture content of 10% and a dry content of 90%, with a protein level of 20%, the calculation would be as follows: 20/0.9 = 22.2% protein on a dry matter basis.

Once the guaranteed analysis has been adjusted, it provides an excellent source of information about the food. But you cannot assess the food alone on the guaranteed analysis; ingredients are also vitally important.

Ingredients

The ingredient list on the label will always be in order of weight. The most important ingredient in a dog food is a meat-based source of protein, so you should look for this as the first ingredient in the list. It is worth bearing in mind, though, that meals, such as turkey meal, have 300% more protein than fresh meat, and therefore it can be the main source of protein despite being very light in weight. In this case, it might be further down the ingredients list.

The most common meat ingredients in dog food are beef, chicken, turkey, lamb, and salmon. These are all excellent sources of protein; however, they are also common allergens. If your dog has an allergy to food, then it's best to look for a food which has an uncommon source of protein, such as duck, venison, or tuna, as they are less likely to react to these. Just because a food says it is salmon flavor, though, does not mean that salmon is the only meat, so always read the label.

Photo Courtesy of
Julie & Holly Simmons
PrairieWyn Golden Retrievers

Fish proteins are particularly high in omega fatty acids, which as mentioned earlier are excellent for the health of both the coat and joints. This is a major benefit for Golden Retrievers.

When it comes to fillers, some pet food manufacturers use grains, some use vegetables, some use both. Grains are excellent sources of fiber and B vitamins; however, some dogs have sensitive guts when it comes to digesting grains. The best grains to look for are whole grains, such as brown rice, barley, and oatmeal. White rice and maize meal are not as nutritional as the whole grains.

Vegetables are far more beneficial to dogs than grains, and potatoes, sweet potatoes, carrots, and peas are all common ingredients. They are great sources of vitamins and minerals, such as vitamin A, B, and C, as well as potassium, iron, and magnesium. Vitamin A aids in keeping the eyes, skin, and brain in good health. Vitamin B works mainly with cell metabolism. Vitamin C helps keep the immune system working efficiently, ready to fight an infection. Potassium is involved in the conduction of signals along nerves as well as keeping the heart beating in a normal rhythm. Magnesium helps develop strong and healthy bones. And finally, iron is used to create red blood cells which carry oxygen around the body.

Weight Monitoring

Golden Retrievers have a hearty appetite, but this doesn't mean that they need a large number of calories. They can be prone to becoming overweight, so choosing a food which is specific to Golden Retrievers, or that is slightly lower in calories without losing quality, might be best suited to your dog.

Being overweight is severely detrimental to joints of Golden Retrievers. As they age, abnormal forces on normal joints will cause arthritis to develop. Because Golden Retrievers are prone to hip and elbow dysplasia, abnormal forces on abnormal joints will cause them to deteriorate very quickly.

There is not a specific weight that a Golden Retriever should be, as each dog is an individual, so the weight is best measured by body condition scoring (BCS). BCS is based on a scale of 1-9, with 5 being the ideal weight, 1 is emaciated, and 9 is obese.

BCS 1 = Emaciated. Ribs, lumbar vertebral projections, and bony prominences around the pelvis are clearly visible. There is severe loss of muscle and no body fat.

BCS 3 = Underweight. Ribs can be felt with ease and might be visible. Not much fat present. The abdomen tucks up at the flank and a waist can be seen from the top. Some bony projections can be seen. Easy to see top of lumbar vertebrae.

BCS 5 = Ideal. Minimal fat over the ribs and can easily feel them. Waist and ribs are visible when standing above the dog. Tucked abdomen when viewed from the side.

BCS 7 = Overweight. Fat present over ribs and need some pressure to feel them. Fat deposits over rump and around tail base. Cannot easily view waist. Abdominal tuck present but slight.

BCS 9 = Obese. Lots of fat around the base of tail, spine, and chest. Abdomen may bulge behind the ribs. No waist or abdominal tuck. Fat deposits on neck and limbs.

Because the Golden Retriever has a glorious thick coat, the best way to measure BCS is with a hands-on approach. This way you will get a good feel about how much fat there is present on your dog. Staying in shape will be greatly beneficial to him so if you need assistance in achieving the ideal weight, most vet practices will run weight clinics with veterinary nurses to provide professional advice and support.

CHAPTER 9
Dental Care

Importance of Dental Care

Just as it is important to keep our own teeth clean, it is equally important to keep the teeth of your dog clean. The diets of our domestic dogs are nothing like the wild diet of their ancestors, and therefore they do not have raw bones to gnaw on, on a daily basis. This is one of the driving factors for the BARF diet as discussed in Chapter 8; however, we have already learned of the dangers of this diet and therefore alternative methods of dental hygiene need to be considered.

Without daily dental care, most dogs will end up needing some sort of intervention later in life to improve the health of their teeth. Poor dental health will lead to mouth pain and bad breath, also known as halitosis, which is not pleasant for your dog. Golden Retrievers in particular are known for their bad breath, but this can be avoided with due diligence.

Dental Anatomy

The tooth structure is so much more than what you see above the gums. The visible tooth is known as the crown and under the gums, the bottom of the tooth is known as the root. The root can be as big as, sometimes bigger, than the crown.

The tooth is made out of bone with several different layers. On the outside is a protective layer called the enamel. This can be worn down through chewing stones and sticks, so it is wise to discourage your Golden from these habits. In the very center of the tooth is the pulp. This is an area filled with nerve endings, so if the teeth wear down to this area, it can be very sore.

To hold the tooth in the socket, there are periodontal ligaments, which are extremely strong ligaments. If the tooth becomes diseased, these ligaments can become weak, which in turn makes the tooth become wobbly and fall out. Eating with a wobbly tooth can be very painful.

Dogs have 42 adult teeth, but initially start off with 28 deciduous (baby) teeth. These baby teeth fall out between 6 months and 18 months of age. You probably won't see them fall out, but you might notice your Golden being a little more mouthy than usual during this time, so plenty of chew toys will help him through the mild discomforts of teething.

The teeth at the front are called the incisors. These are for picking meat off bones. The next are the canines, which are long and sharp. They would originally have been the teeth used to hunt and bite down on their prey. The teeth on the insides of the cheek are called pre-molars and molars. These are crushing teeth. Combined with the power of the masticatory jaw muscles, they can potentially crunch through bones.

Tartar Build-Up and Gingivitis

Photo Courtesy of Bruno Rosales

Tartar is a build-up of food and bacteria around the base of the tooth. This happens in all dogs who do not have their teeth brushed on a daily basis. Tartar leads to halitosis and therefore also a poor taste in your dog's mouth.

Due to tartar build-up, your dog is also likely to have gingivitis. This is an inflammation of the gums, local to where the tartar builds up. The reason why the gums become inflamed is because the tartar is full of bacteria. Therefore, the body sends white blood cells to the area to fight the bacteria, but the influx of white blood cells causes the area to swell.

When this happens, the only way this can be reversed is to remove the tartar. Antibiotics and anti-inflammatories will temporary relieve the problem; however, the body will continue to respond in this manner to the tartar, and therefore, the gingivitis and halitosis will come straight back.

Dental Care

Examining

Keeping a close eye on your dog's dental health is a vital part of care for your dog. Early detection will ensure prevention of major dental disease as your dog ages.

The best way to examine your dog's teeth is on a day he's feeling happy and relaxed. If he feels nervous or in a bad mood, you might make things worse by examining things, and while it's not in the nature for a Golden Retriever to snap, it's worth being careful since you are working with the mouth.

HELPFUL TIP
Make Toothbrushing Part of your Daily Routine

Did you know that four out of five dogs have periodontal disease by the time they're three years old? Periodontal disease causes more than just bad breath and brown teeth—bacteria under the gumline can travel throughout your Golden Retriever's bloodstream and cause life-threatening health problems. Make toothbrushing part of your daily routine to help your Golden live a long, healthy life.

Start by lifting up the front lips and looking at the incisors. They should be white or cream in color with minimal tartar. They should not be wobbly and the gums should not be receding. The next ones to look at are the canines. These build up a lot of tartar easily. Then finally pull the cheeks right back to view the pre-molars and molars. It's a common mistake not to pull the cheeks back far enough to view the very back teeth so be aware of this. Luckily, Goldens have fairly big jowls and a bit of slack in this area makes it easier.

If you see a tooth which is gray and much darker than the rest, it is a sign that it is dying from the inside pulp area, and even if it is not wobbly or covered in tartar, your veterinarian should assess the tooth.

Every time you take your dog to the vet, they should have their teeth investigated in this manner; however, making a mental note each time you brush, and once a month making a conscious effort to thoroughly check the mouth, will make sure you pick up on any abnormalities early.

Tooth Brushing

Tooth brushing may seem a strange thing to do to your dog, but your dog will be grateful in the long run for it. Tooth brushing daily from a young age will prevent tooth decay, gingivitis, and tartar build-up.

Photo Courtesy of Melissa Morrison

Always brush your dog's teeth with a dog toothpaste, as human toothpaste often contains a sweetener called xylitol. This is extremely dangerous to your dog as it can cause their blood glucose to drastically drop. This in turn will cause seizures and potentially even lead to death. Dog toothpaste contains many enzymes, which specifically dissolve off the tartar from the tooth. Once the tartar has become extensive, though, it will not solve the problem, but it will stop it from worsening.

The Golden Retriever is a big dog, so you can brush his mouth with a small human toothbrush, or purchase a dog toothbrush. The benefit of a dog toothbrush is that it is angled so that brushing the back teeth is easier. You can also use a rubber finger brush, which looks a little like a large thimble, if this is easier for you.

If you train your dog from a puppy to be tolerant of his teeth being brushed, you will have much less hassle throughout your dog's life, versus if you start at a later stage. Some dogs resent the manipulation to some degree, so training from a puppy will teach him it is a fun process. Ensure you give him lots of praise afterward with toys or treats, whichever he prefers.

Water Additives

There are several water additives available to buy from pet stores and veterinary practices. These act like mouthwash for dogs. You can add the specified amount to fresh water daily, and it helps to freshen the breath and dissolve anything accumulating on the teeth.

These should be used in addition to brushing and not instead of, as the manual brushing of the brush will be far more effective than a fluid running over the teeth. Like toothpaste, however, it is full of enzymes and works in a similar manner.

It is very important, though, that you do not use human mouthwash. It is markedly different, and if you were to put human mouthwash in the water, it could cause serious poisoning and internal damage to your dog.

Chews

It is difficult to choose appropriate chews with so much choice on the market. Every manufacturer claims their treat is the most effective, but in the end, the best thing to do is simply find one your dog likes.

Dental chews work by causing mild abrasion as they are bitten through. It will either help remove tartar through sucking it off or cracking it off. There are many different sizes and shapes of treats available. Your Golden Retriever will need one which is fairly large. Too little and it might not remove the tartar appropriately.

Dental chews should be given as part of your dog's daily diet and not in addition to it. Therefore, if your dog needs 1,000 calories per day and the treat is 150 calories, then make sure you subtract that amount of food from the daily quantity recommended.

Some owners prefer knuckle bones to commercial treats, and while they are far more natural than processed chews, they come with some significant hazards. Knuckle bones may shatter and cause trauma to the intestines or stomach, and if large bits are broken off which are small enough to swallow, your dog may develop a life-threatening intestinal blockage.

If you would like a natural dental chew which is less hazardous, then antlers are an excellent alternative. The slow gnawing of the hard antler helps remove the tartar. Antlers do not shatter like knuckle bones and take an extremely long time to wear down, therefore are great long-lasting alternatives to other dental chews available.

Dental Food

Many of the top dog food brands have created dental diets. These are dry dog foods with large kibble bits in them. As the dog bites through the kibble, it helps remove the tartar from the teeth. The kibble pieces are usually a tiny bit softer than other dry dog foods, so that as the tooth is removed from the kibble, there is a small amount of suction.

Dental formulated diets are not completely necessary to maintain good dental health. They are mainly marketed at dogs who have dental disease. For Goldens whose owners wish to prevent dental disease, a normal quality dry dog food for large dogs will suffice.

Dental Procedures

If the mouth is in very bad health, your veterinarian may suggest having your dog in for a dental procedure. This is a day procedure where your dog will come home the same day.

Dentals require a general anesthetic, as working in that area in a conscious dog is almost impossible. General anesthetics are generally very

Photo Courtesy of
Karan Gogri

safe in a healthy dog; however, if your dog has any kidney or liver disease, your veterinarian may want to check their blood before, and administer intravenous fluids to keep their blood pressure stable.

Once your dog is anesthetized, the vet will start by cracking off any large areas of tartar. He will then scale all the teeth to make them clean and white. Once they are clean, he will take a probe and run it around each tooth. If the probe dips into the socket, then it means that the periodontal ligament has been damaged and the tooth must be removed. Some teeth have multiple roots, and some just a single root. This usually determines how difficult they are to remove. A sharp tool called an elevator is run around the root of the tooth to break the periodontal ligament before the tooth is pulled out. The socket is sometimes stitched closed afterward, although some veterinarians prefer leaving it open. At the end of the procedure, the veterinarian will polish the entire mouth to remove any residual tartar.

Dental procedures sound invasive; however, if your dog has a mouth full of bacteria, he will be glad for the procedure. It will restore comfort and remove bad breath. Nevertheless, dental procedures can be avoided altogether with routine care of your Golden's teeth so try to make it a habit from a very young age to preserve the health of the mouth.

CHAPTER 10
Grooming

About the Coat

Golden Retrievers have a beautiful wavy golden coat, which can vary in color. When a Golden is still a puppy, it is likely to be much lighter than their adult coat color. You may be able to have an indication of what your puppy's adult coat may look like by the color of his ear tips. But it will darken as your dog reaches adulthood, and then may lighten up again slightly toward his twilight years.

The coat is medium in length, apart from some areas of feathering around the neck, back of legs, tail, and under the body. These are longer areas of hair. Your Golden Retriever has a "double coat," which means that there is an undercoat. This aids in keeping your dog warm in the winter months. When the weather warms up in summer, the undercoat sheds, which is known as "blowing the coat."

The coat can look striking, and while it does need regular management to keep it in good condition, it does not require you to rush off to the groomer every week to keep up appearances.

Photo Courtesy of
Angie Wrightstone

Coat Health

The coat of a Golden is prone to excessive shedding, especially in the summer months when the undercoat is coming out. As a result, brushing your dog daily will help keep your house from becoming covered in fur. By doing this, you will be removing all the loose hair in the brush, instead of letting it fall to the floor.

Brushing the coat needs to be done at least once per week, ideally more like daily, but it can be done with relative ease. A useful tip to consider when grooming is to take your dog outside, as there may be a large amount of loose hair that comes out. The grooming routine should be introduced from a young age as some dogs do not like the fuss when it is only introduced later in life.

When starting out with grooming, you must first consider what tools you might need. The most common brush to buy is a slicker brush. This has a large surface area and is covered in fine pins. These brushes are

HELPFUL TIP
Coat Care

Did you know that a Golden Retriever's coat helps it keep cool in addition to keeping it warm? Shaving exposes your dog's skin to direct sunlight, which makes it heat up faster. It also doesn't reduce shedding; it only shortens the length of hair shed. Not only that, but repeated shaving could ruin your Golden's coat, especially if it develops a health condition like hypothyroidism. Instead of shaving your Golden, go for a deshedding service and a short feather trim. A groomer can also shave your dog's belly so it can feel the coolness of grass or tile more easily.

excellent for working through loose hair, especially when it is slightly matted.

The next tool you will need is a steel comb of a good quality. These are for going through the coat after the slicker brush, to ensure it is completely knot free. They are commonly referred to as Greyhound combs. They sometimes have wide- and narrow-spaced prongs all on one comb, or are available as individual combs, however with a Golden Retriever, it is not essential that you buy the smallest ones.

Golden groomers usually have a set of scissors and thinning shears in their grooming kit also. The coat of a Golden Retriever does not need to be routinely cut, but it does help to occasionally style the wayward areas. The thinning shears look like a cross between scissors and a comb. These are excellent for debulking heavy areas of fur. You may notice there are other tools to cope with shedding, such as stripping knives or shedding blades, but professional Golden Retriever groomers rarely use these heavy-duty tools. A slicker brush and thinning shears should be enough to keep on top of the thick shedding coat without damaging it.

Your local groomer will be able to help with grooming your Golden if you feel like keeping on top of his big coat will be too much of a task. Groomers will always bathe your dog before brushing their coat, which will help to detangle any areas of stubborn fur. However, this does not need to be done on a daily basis when grooming at home. In fact, it is detrimental to the coat to wash it too often as it will strip it of the natural oils. A rinse-down with water after a muddy walk is fine, but shampooing should only be done when necessary, and not more frequently than once a month, unless advised by your vet for medical reasons.

There are many different shampoos on the market, and as long as your Golden doesn't have any skin allergies, most will be fine to use. However, if you wish to choose one which is gentle and nourishing, then oatmeal-based shampoos are excellent. Also, shampoos containing tea-tree have anti-inflammatory and anti-bacterial properties too.

External Parasites

There are many creepy crawlies that love to live in your dog's coat, the most common of which are fleas; however, you may find mites, lice, and ticks in there too. All of these are picked up in the environment and from other animals.

Fleas actually prefer to live 90% of the time in the environment and only 10% of the time on your dog, and once your dog has brought them into the house, they can breed extremely quickly. Therefore, if your dog has a flea problem, ensure you not only treat him, but also wash all his bedding in hot water, and vacuum and spray with an insecticide all the areas of the house which are dark and warm. Examples of these places include under the sofas and down the back of cushions.

Ticks can be picked up when walking your dog in areas where there are deer or long grass. They suck blood and become engorged before falling off. They should be removed when first noticed because they have the potential to cause a nasty skin infection in the region of the bite, and in rare scenarios, they can transmit very serious diseases. Ticks can be removed with a tick twister, which is a small fork you place around the base of the body, then twist and pull. This motion ensures the head has not been left in, which may cause infection.

Most external parasite treatments will treat for fleas, in combination with mites, lice, and/or ticks, so reading the label is vital, since they are not all the same. Flea treatments should be applied on a routine basis as directed by your vet, to provide protection against external parasites. Prevention is always better than cure. These treatments can come in a variety of forms to suit your and your dog, such as spot-on pipettes, tablets, treats, and shampoos.

Nail Clipping

"Touch their paws and feet frequently so they get used to you handling their paws for trimming their toenails. Ideally you should trim their nails every two weeks."

Lori Reuter
Avalor Goldens

Dogs have four nails on each paw, and on the front leg there is also a dew claw on the inside. Some dogs may have dew claws on the inside of their back legs too, but this is unusual. All these nails will need to be routinely clipped to keep short as they can have the tendency to grow in a curved manner, which then results in them damaging the underside of the paw, or being susceptible to being caught and causing toe sprains and dislocations.

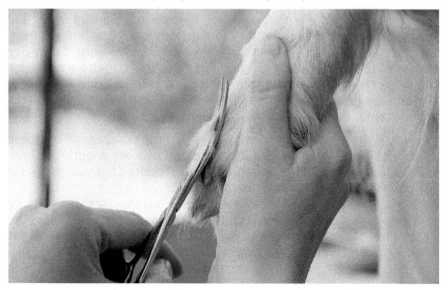

Clipping nails can cause some dogs great anxiety, so teaching your dog to be still and not panic when they are young is a good idea. Start as a puppy by playing with their paws and giving them plenty of praise when they do not fuss. Since Golden Retrievers are dogs that want to please, they are easier than other breeds to get used to nail clipping.

You can buy dog nail clippers from most pet stores, and these are far superior to using human nail clippers, especially since Golden Retrievers have large, thick nails, which can take quite a lot of strength to get through. There are lots of sizes to choose from, but you will need the biggest for your Golden.

The nail is made up of keratin, which does not contain nerves or blood vessels, so if you clip the nail correctly, it will not cause any pain to your dog. However, running down the center of the nail is a fleshy section called the quick. If you accidentally cut the quick, it will bleed profusely. While your dog will not bleed out from this, stopping the bleeding is in the best interests of both your dog and the floor! Simply apply firm pressure to it with a wad of cotton wool for five minutes to get it under control.

Knowing where the quick ends is usually a guessing game for dogs with black nails, but if you are lucky to have a dog with clear nails, then it can easily be seen. For dogs with black nails, taking small bits off at a time, rather than one big cut, is a better idea. If you are nervous about cutting your dog's nails, a groomer or a veterinary nurse will be more than happy to help you out.

Ear Cleaning

The ear is made up of several sections. The flap, which we most commonly refer to as the ear, is called the pinna. Since Goldens have a pinna which flops down, the inside of the ear is prone to becoming moist, which maintains an excellent environment for bacteria and yeast to grow in. Unfortunately, this does mean they can be susceptible to ear infections. Cleaning the ears weekly, or after every swim, will ensure that the inside of the ear is kept clean.

The inside of the ear is made up of several sections. The first section of the external ear canal is called the vertical canal, which travels down toward the ground and then turns 90 degrees and travels into the head toward the brain. This section is called the horizontal canal. It is met by the tympanic membrane at the end, which is a very small sheet of tissue. If this becomes ruptured, then infections can travel deeper into the ear and become serious. After the tympanic membrane is the middle ear, followed by the inner ear. Infections in these regions can affect balance and are extremely painful, whereas infections in just the outer ear will be very itchy and cause scratching and shaking of the head.

Your veterinarian will be able to sell you some ear cleaner which they approve of. The signs you are looking out for when it comes to a general ear cleaner are that it is gentle, it maintains the pH of the ear, and it helps loosen or dissolve waxy accumulations.

To clean the ear, all you need to do is lift up the pinna of the ear, place the nozzle of the ear cleaner as deep into the vertical ear canal as you can, and give a squeeze. When you remove it from the ear canal, quickly place the pinna of the ear over the exit to the canal so that none can come out, and give the area a massage for about 30 seconds. This allows the ear cleaner to do its work and loosen the wax. When you let go, take a step back, as your dog will want to shake his head. This is a good thing as it gets out all the ear cleaner and wax, but it can be messy and you don't want to be in the firing line! Once he has finished shaking his head, take some cotton wool and wipe clean everything that has come out.

Anal Glands

Some dogs suffer from anal gland impactions, while others may go their whole lives without having their anal glands emptied. Anal glands are two small sac-like structures that sit on the inside of the anus, in the 4 and 8 o'clock positions. As the dog passes a stool, these are naturally squeezed and anything in them will be emptied. They are redundant structures with no functional use, and if they become recurrent problems, some owners opt to remove them.

HELPFUL TIP
Brushing is Crucial

Many people think Golden Retrievers have low-maintenance coats, but the truth is that in addition to shedding, they are prone to matting behind the ears and in their butt feathers. Brushing your Golden at least once a week (and daily during shedding season) not only reduces how much hair gets on your furniture and floats around your house but also helps prevent painful mats.

Dogs start having problems with anal glands for one of three reasons; the most common reason is a malposition of them. Instead of them being located at 4 and 8 o'clock, they might be in the 3 and 9 o'clock positions, which means as the dog defecates, they are not emptied efficiently. The second reason is when the dog has loose stools. In this instance, the stool doesn't push on the anal glands as it passes, and the very watery parts may even fill the anal glands up. The final cause of anal gland problems is due to tumors which can grow in that region. These can cause the anal glands to fill up with inflammatory cells.

The most common sign you will see, if your dog is experiencing discomfort with his anal glands, is rubbing his bottom along the floor. This is called scooting. Other signs you might notice are licking the area and a fishy smell coming from your dog. If you think your dog needs his anal glands emptying, you should take him to your vet or groomer to express them. It is not an emergency, but taking the approach that they might sort themselves out is not advisable, as anal glands which are full can quickly lead to abscesses, which are much harder to treat.

Golden Retrievers are beautiful dogs, and by following the advice in this chapter, you will certainly help keep your Golden in tiptop condition. Not only will he look great, but he will feel great too.

CHAPTER 11
Preventative Veterinary Medicine

Choosing a Veterinarian

Once you have acquired your new puppy or dog, it is important to make acquaintances with your local veterinarian. It can be difficult to choose which veterinarian to go to, but there are a few things to keep in mind when looking around.

Location

The proximity to your home is an important factor to consider. While this may not make much of an impact when you are taking your dog for his yearly check-up, you will be grateful for the proximity in the event of a life-threatening emergency. Timely arrival at your veterinarian may be the difference between life and death for your dog.

Finances

Veterinarians can charge competitive prices, so you will find that some are cheaper than others. Large corporate companies will often have specials every month to promote different aspects of health. Many vet practices will also offer a pet plan, which involves a monthly payment and in return it may include discounted visits and products, and low cost or free annual check-ups, parasite prevention, and vaccinations.

After-hours services

Some veterinary practices will offer their own after-hours emergency services to their clients, while others will dedicate their emergency services to an external provider. If continuity is important to you, then finding a veterinary practice who provides these services for their clients is the best, as they will know your dog and have your records in their filing system. However, a benefit of an external provider is the experience they can bring with them. Most external after-hours services will have veterinarians who are dedicated emergency vets, with further qualifications in the critical care field, and therefore, in the case of an emergency, they will have more experience with making decisions under pressure.

Specialties

While all veterinarians have to go through extensive training to become a vet, some will receive post-graduate qualifications as well. These might be in fields such as ophthalmology, orthopedics, cardiology, or dermatology to name a few. A general veterinarian will always be able to refer your dog to these specialists; however, for some owners, it is important to have access to specialists at their own vet practice.

Extras

Some vet practices will also offer extra services such as grooming services, veterinary nurse consults, boarding, weight clinics, and puppy classes. When choosing a veterinary practice, it is worth considering if these factors are ones you would like to have available to you.

Vaccinations

It is vitally important that you vaccinate your dog from a puppy. There are dangerous canine diseases commonly found, which may threaten the health and even the life of your dog. Luckily these diseases can easily be vaccinated against.

Vaccinations should be started at 8 weeks old, or if the dog you are acquiring is older than this, as soon as possible. The initial vaccination course will be two or three vaccinations, several weeks apart, depending on which manufacturer your veterinarian uses. Most vets will vaccinate against five diseases as compulsory, and give an additional vaccination as an option.

Parvovirus is a disease which affects mainly puppies, although any age can contract it. It is a deadly virus which causes bleeding into the guts and diarrhea. Some dogs may also vomit. This leads to rapid dehydration. It is picked up in the environment, mainly through fecal-oral transmission, or sharing of food and water bowls.

Hepatitis, otherwise known as canine adenovirus, is a disease which affects the liver. The inflammation in the liver can cause a fever, vomiting, lethargy, diarrhea, jaundice, and enlarged lymph nodes, and eventually leads to death.

Distemper is a virus which affects many different body systems. It initially causes vomiting, sneezing, and coughing, as well as thickened pads on the paws and the tip of the nose. Once the virus has spread to the brain it causes seizures.

Photo Courtesy of
Bruno Rosales

Leptospirosis is a disease which has several different serotypes. Some vets vaccinate against the two most common ones, some vaccinate against four. It can cause similar symptoms to hepatitis, such as vomiting, diarrhea, and jaundice, but it also will cause neurological symptoms. It mainly affects the kidneys, liver, central nervous system, and reproductive system.

Kennel cough is a disease which is vaccinated against by squirting the vaccine up the nose. Kennel cough is actually a complex of diseases, which are commonly caused by Bordetella and Parainfluenza in combination. Kennel cough causes a harsh goose-honk or hacking cough, and may cause phlegm to be brought up. It can easily be mistaken for vomiting.

Rabies is the final vaccination which is vital in areas of the world where it is endemic. Rabies is a disease which affects the brain, and is spread through saliva which has contaminated blood. This may be through bites, or simply saliva contaminating a scratch. It is transmissible to humans, which is why it is so important.

Distemper, hepatitis, and parvovirus are often combined into one injectable vaccination, which is sometimes also combined with leptospirosis and possibly parainfluenza in one syringe. If parainfluenza isn't given in the injectable form, it can be combined with Bordetella in a vaccine which squirts up the nose. Rabies, however, is given as an individual injectable vaccination.

Some dog owners do not believe in vaccinations, and therefore do not wish to have their dogs vaccinated; however, vaccinations are extremely safe and the prevalence of side effects is extremely low. It is advised that a puppy has at least the initial course of vaccines and the booster at one year old, but after that, if an owner does not wish to vaccinate, then blood tests can be done yearly to investigate the levels of immunity. That way, the dog only needs to receive vaccinations when the immunity dips, rather than every year.

Microchipping

Microchipping is recommended for all dogs, and in the UK, it has now become a legal requirement. It is not yet a legal requirement in the USA, but it is highly recommended. A microchip is a small piece of metal which is inserted under the skin in between the shoulder blades. When it is scanned by a reader, it gives a number, which can then be looked up with the microchip company. The number is unique and your details will be registered to the number so it is important to remember to update them if you move house or change cell phone numbers.

It is inserted with a needle, a bit like an injection, which might make your dog yelp briefly, but the pain is very short-lived. The veterinarian will ensure the area between the shoulder blades is clean before inserting it. Golden Retrievers are a brave breed, so if you are having a microchip inserted into an adult dog, they probably will not react at all.

Neutering

If you are not planning on breeding your Golden Retriever, it is for the benefit of their health to get them neutered. For female dogs, this is called spaying, and for male dogs, it is called castration. There are pros and cons of both, but for most dogs, the pros outweigh the cons vastly.

The procedures for both males and females require just a day visit to the vet. You will need to bring in your dog early in the morning, having not had breakfast, and the operation will usually be done by lunchtime. They will then spend the afternoon recovering and sleeping off the remainder of the anesthetic before being allowed home.

Spaying

A female dog can be spayed any time in its life, however, most vets agree that it should either be done before the first season, or three months after the first season. This will be around a year of age, give or take a few months. As mentioned in Chapter 1, there are benefits for waiting until one year old for Golden Retrievers, as the hormones aid closure of the bone growth plates. However, if she is spayed before the first season, the chances of mammary cancer later in life is almost nil. This is because mammary cancers are driven by hormones, and if she has never had a season, she has not ever been exposed to high levels of hormones.

On the other hand, a positive of certain hormones, estrogen in particular, is that it helps tighten the urethral sphincter. This is a band of muscle that closes the exit to the bladder and if it becomes weak and leaky, then the dog might start leaking urine when lying down in particular. This usually only becomes evident in older age though. Not all female dogs spayed after the first season will develop this, but it is a risk factor to consider.

A dog should not be spayed within the three months after a season. This is because the uterus will be very swollen and therefore it could be a

Photo Courtesy of
Karan Gogri

difficult and risky operation. Also, another negative is that the hormones will still be high in the system and therefore a spay operation too close to the season may cause a phantom pregnancy.

Despite all these points, spaying is extremely beneficial for the dog as it eliminates the risk of pyometra (uterine infection), uterine cancers, and ovarian cancers. These are all life-threatening.

Castration

The castration operation is much easier than the spay operation, and significantly quicker too. Castrating a dog will eliminate the chance of testicular and epidydimal cancers, and significantly reduce the risk of prostate hyperplasia (enlargement) and prostate cancer.

Castrating a dog will also help control unwanted behavior too. He is less likely to roam or run away, and aggression will be significantly reduced.

Castration operations can be done any time from when two testicles have descended into the scrotum. This may be from just a few months old; however, it is recommended that your dog is at least six months old, or even over a year for Goldens as mentioned previously, as young puppies can have a sudden drop in glucose levels when they are operated on which can make recovery a slower process.

Internal Parasites

Parasite control is vital for the health of your dog. External parasite control is discussed in Chapter 10, but internal parasites must also be controlled.

Internal parasites mainly consist of roundworms and tapeworms; however, heartworm and protozoa such as Giardia also need to be considered. Treatment, obtained from your veterinarian, given every three months will aid in avoiding these infections. However, if you live in a lungworm endemic area, it is advisable to de-worm monthly to avoid your Golden Retriever contracting this.

Internal parasites can be picked up from scavenging on walks, coming into contact with other dogs or their feces, sharing bowls, or drinking dirty water. The exception is lungworm, which is contracted through eating snails or slugs. Golden Retrievers love picking up things on walks, so being vigilant about what your dog is doing will reduce the chances of him picking up parasites.

Pet Insurance

Pet insurance will aid in covering potential veterinary bills which can total thousands of dollars. Many people will not have that in savings and vets usually require payment upfront before discharge of the animal.

There are several different policy types which are available, so reading the fine print carefully and selecting the option which works best for you will be in your best interests. Some insurance companies give you a sum of money per condition, which renews every year, whereas some companies will provide a sum of money per condition for the whole lifetime. Other companies will give you a sum of money for all health care which renews every year.

In addition to this, the co-payment will differ from company to company, and a higher co-payment might reduce the annual payment; however, it will require for you to pay more toward the claim. Also, some insurers will also require you to pay a percentage of the fee if your dog is over a certain age.

Nevertheless, pet insurance will save you a great deal of money long term if anything happens to your dog, and will allow your vet to provide him with the gold standard vet care without financial concerns.

HELPFUL TIP
Pet Insurance

Unfortunately, Golden Retrievers are prone to a lot of health issues and are one of the breeds most plagued by cancer (61 percent of Goldens die from cancer). Pet insurance can help with some of the costs associated with these health problems, but it doesn't cover preexisting conditions, and there are often waiting periods before coverage begins. Therefore, you should consider signing up for pet insurance as soon as you bring your Golden Retriever home so you never have to decide whether or not you can afford to save your pup's life.

In the end, if you provide excellent preventative veterinary care for your dog, he will love you for it, as he will be as healthy as can be, and what is better than a happy, healthy Golden Retriever?

CHAPTER 12
Golden Retriever Diseases

"Goldens share several genetic worries. A specific eye disease called pigmentary uveitis (or colloquially Golden Retriever Uveitis) is a serious affliction. Specific cancers, especially Hemangiosarcoma, is a worry for golden lovers. SAS is a heart condition better controlled now than in the past, but really needs breeders who have done their cardiac clearances for breeding dogs."

Jill Simmons
PoeticGold Farm

NOT-SO-FUN FACTS
Common Health Problems

Sadly, Golden Retrievers are prone to a variety of health problems. In addition to the fact that more than half of all Goldens die from cancer, other common health problems include:

- Hip or elbow dysplasia
- Progressive Retinal Atrophy (PRA)
- Cataracts
- Osteochondrosis Dissecans (OCD)
- Subvalvular Aortic Stenosis
- Allergies
- Bloat
- Von Willebrand's Disease
- Hypothyroidism
- Epilepsy

While all owners strive to have a happy, healthy dog, unfortunately there are some genetic diseases which no matter how healthy your dog is, they stand a chance of contracting. However, just because the breed is predisposed to a certain condition, does not mean that your dog will definitely suffer from it at some point in his life. When you are a Golden Retriever owner, there are some conditions which you should have heightened awareness about, so that if you notice the symptoms, you can see your vet sooner rather than later. That way, your dog will get the best treatment as early as possible, to stop the progression of the disease soon after it starts.

*Photo Courtesy of
Kellie Blood*

Cardiac Diseases

Aortic Stenosis

Also known as subaortic stenosis (SAS), this is a heart condition which causes a narrowing of the exit to the heart. The left-hand side of the heart pumps oxygenated blood coming back from the lungs to the body, so when the exit is narrowed there will be more resistance, and therefore the heart muscle must contract significantly harder to push the blood out.

Like any muscle that works hard, it will gradually grow bigger. But unlike muscles in other parts of the body, where big muscles mean strong muscles, the heart cannot cope well when it is enlarged. As a result, the blood backs up on this side of the heart to the lungs, which is where it is coming from. An increased pressure in the backed-up blood will cause fluid to leak out of the vein into the surrounding tissues, in this case the lungs. So, in severe cases the lungs will become filled with fluid and the dog will cough. The other symptom it may demonstrate is lethargy or fainting due to not enough oxygenated blood being pumped to the other parts of the body.

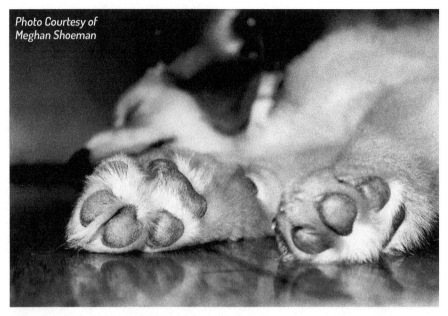

Photo Courtesy of
Meghan Shoeman

Apart from clinical symptoms, it is diagnosed through an ultrasound scan of the heart. If it's caught early, a veterinary cardiologist can treat this condition to widen the exit of the heart, which will significantly improve the life of the dog. However, if diagnosed late in the disease process, when the heart has already enlarged and the lungs are already compromised, then there are excellent medications to decrease the blood pressure, put less stress on the heart, and decrease any fluid in the lungs.

Pericardial Effusion

The heart is surrounded by a tissue sac called the pericardium. When this fills up with fluid, it constricts the heart's ability to pump effectively. While both sides are affected, the right-hand side of the heart has thinner walls, and therefore it can become more compromised than the left. The blood coming to the right-hand side of the heart is from the body, so that it can be pumped to the lungs to become oxygenated again. If this blood backs up on its journey to the heart, it may leak fluid out of the vessels into the abdominal cavity.

The cause of pericardial effusions is occasionally cancerous in origin; most commonly a tumor on the outside of the heart. However, it can also be idiopathic, meaning of unknown origin. There was a study in a UK veterinary hospital looking at 143 cases of pericardial effusions, of which

47 cases were Golden Retrievers. Within those 47 cases, seven had a tumor, and the other 40 had no known cause.

Your vet will have a suspicion of pericardial effusion if your dog has suddenly become very lethargic or started fainting or coughing, as when he listens to the heart, it will have the sound of a washing machine, rather than a beating sound. This can be confirmed with either an ultrasound or X-ray. Most vets will be able to drain the fluid from around the heart in a general practice; unfortunately, if the cause is due to cancer, it is likely to simply refill again. Nevertheless, if it is of idiopathic origin, draining the pericardium may be curative.

Dermatological Diseases

Atopic Dermatitis

There are varied opinions as to whether Golden Retrievers are at increased risk of skin allergies, otherwise known as atopic dermatitis, and it appears that it varies between geographical locations.

Skin allergies can be due to several potential causes; food, the environment, or bites. When your dog has a flare-up, he will be extremely itchy, and may scratch and lick various parts of his body such as his feet, underarms, belly, and the inside of his hind legs. He may also have a flare-up of his ear canals and shake his head excessively to relieve his itchy ears.

If you are treating regularly for external parasites to prevent them, then the allergy is unlikely to be due to these, but they should be ruled out with a vet check. A flea allergy only needs one bite to cause your dog to be itchy.

Photo Courtesy of Ashley DeFrancesco

Food allergies should be ruled out first with an elimination diet. These are available from your veterinarian. These diets have had all the protein molecules hydrolyzed, which means the body cannot recognize them to react to them. This diet should be fed for six weeks, with no treats or table scraps. If your dog has significantly improved, then different flavors of meat should gradually be introduced again to see what causes the allergy to flare up.

If both parasites and food allergies have been ruled out, the remaining cause is the environment. This could be due to contact with an allergen, such as floor cleaner or long grass, or inhalant, such as pollen. These allergies are difficult to get on top of as they cannot be avoided. There are several treatment options, which focus on three things; treat flare-ups, prevent future flare-ups, and maintain the health of the coat. Allergies cannot be cured.

There are several different tablets available from your vet to aid the itchiness. Steroids are by far the cheapest, but have major side effects as well as putting a lot of strain on the liver. There are other options which downregulate the immune response to the allergens, but they are costlier.

Another option is for your veterinarian to formulate a vaccination against the allergen. This is administered in increasing intervals, for example firstly at 2 days apart then 4, then a week, etc. These are effective for many dogs; however, the response is not instant.

Finally, diets containing omega-3 and omega-6 should complement any therapy. In the right ratio, they have pronounced anti-inflammatory effects. They also help build up the lipid layer of the skin to provide a better barrier against external allergens.

Wet Eczema

Wet eczema is also known as acute moist dermatitis or hot spots. Golden Retrievers have a higher incidence of contracting wet eczema and dogs under the age of four are at increased risk.

It is simply an area of bacterial infection which is red, oozy, and extremely itchy. Your dog will want to lick the area constantly but this is counterproductive as it will cause the infection to spread much quicker. Often the wet eczema is far more extensive than the owner realizes due to the thick coat of a Golden Retriever.

Your vet will be able to recognize it immediately, and will begin by clipping away the hair to reveal the extent of it, as well as let the fresh air get to the area. He will clean the area with antiseptic, which you will need to continue doing until it begins to resolve. Your dog will need a long course of antibiotics—often several weeks' worth—as well as wear a buster collar around his neck to stop him from licking.

Hypothyroidism

Hypothyroidism is when the thyroid gland does not work efficiently. This can be for several reasons; however, in the Golden Retriever, it is usually due to a prevalence of thyroid hormone autoantibodies (THAA). These attack the thyroid. The thyroid plays a vital role in metabolism, so a dog with hypothyroidism will be sluggish with an increased weight despite a reduced appetite. He might also have a poor skin barrier and thinner hair, due to increased shedding.

Hypothyroidism cannot be cured but it can be managed very effectively with daily tablets, on which your dog can live a normal life.

Hemangiosarcoma

Golden Retrievers are at an increased risk for a tumor called a hemangiosarcoma. This tumor initially originates on the spleen, but it can spread to the liver, omentum, and lungs. Signs of this tumor are non-specific and you might just notice a sluggishness of your dog and pale gums. A veterinarian, however, will be able to feel a mass in the abdomen, and he may pick it up during a routine check over at an annual vaccination.

Hemangiosarcoma tumors are dangerous, and can cause massive bleeds from the spleen which can lead to sudden death. If the tumor hasn't spread to other organs, the spleen can be removed via surgery. Most general practitioner vets can do this surgery, but it is lengthy and not without risk. Nevertheless, without the surgery, the prognosis is very poor, and therefore many owners will justify going ahead with the operation on that basis. Once operated on, your dog will be able to live a normal life without a spleen.

Joint Diseases

Elbow Dysplasia

Elbow dysplasia is a common cause of lameness in the front limbs in young dogs. Golden Retrievers are at high risk of this condition. Elbow dysplasia is where parts of the elbow, such as the medial coronoid process or anconeal process, haven't developed appropriately, and have become detached.

It is a genetic condition and therefore any breeding dogs should have X-rays to confirm the health of the elbows prior to being bred.

Elbow dysplasia can be improved via joint surgery to remove any fragments. Conservative management is also an option which entails anti-inflammatories when needed, controlled exercise including hydrotherapy, and joint supplements, which are discussed further in Chapter 16.

Hip Dysplasia

Photo Courtesy of Chris Wicks

The hip is made up of a ball and socket joint, where the top of the femur meets the pelvis. The top of the femur should be perfectly round and sit in the socket like a puzzle piece, however when a dog has hip dysplasia, the shapes do not match up. It is usually the ball, rather than the socket which is affected. This can cause the hip to become luxated out of the socket if severe, and causes a swing like gait, and hind limb lameness.

Like elbow dysplasia, hip dysplasia is also of genetic origin, and therefore the parents should be checked prior to breeding. There are several surgical options, such as replacing the hip with an implant, or fusing it if very severe and finances are a problem, however conservative management is more commonly carried out, which is the same as for elbow dysplasia.

Osteochondrosis Dissecans

Osteochondrosis, also known as OCD, is a condition which usually becomes apparent between 4 and 12 months old. The ends of all bones begin as cartilage, but when a puppy has OCD, it doesn't convert to bone. Instead, it becomes thickened cartilage, which can become fragmented, or cause a flap, and as a result, gives rise to considerable joint pain.

The joints affected in Goldens are most commonly the shoulder and stifle, although it can happen in any joint of the limb, and therefore the lameness can either be front or hind limb. It is diagnosed with an X-ray and treated with removal of the loose cartilage via arthroscopy, which involves a small camera to be placed inside the joint.

All the joint conditions of Golden Retrievers are seen in younger dogs; however, they will gradually progress to arthritis if not treated or managed appropriately. Arthritis is further discussed in Chapter 16.

Progressive Retinal Atrophy

Abbreviated to PRA, progressive retinal atrophy is a recessive inherited disease. It can be tested for in breeding animals, and it is the responsible thing to do for anyone intending to breed a Golden.

It causes gradual vision loss, which begins with night blindness. This is due to the back of the eye, known as the retina, gradually deteriorating. There is no treatment for PRA, and it will always lead to blindness of both eyes.

Ectopic Ureters

The ureter is the tube which carries urine from the kidneys to the bladder, where it is stored until there is enough for the dog to void it. The word ectopic means "outside," and ectopic ureters are exactly that. It occurs when the ureters come to an end outside the bladder, usually into the urethra, which is the tube which carries the urine from the bladder to outside the body. As a result, dogs which have ectopic ureters will constantly leak urine.

Generally, it is more common in females, and is usually apparent before one year of age. There is nothing medical which can be done for the condition, and surgery is the only option to correct the anatomical abnormality. While waiting for the surgery, the hair should be kept short around the area where the urine is leaking to avoid urine scald, and the area cleaned regularly.

Photo Courtesy of Heather Dawson

Goldens are prone to many diseases, many of which are genetic in origin, but that is commonly the case with any breed of pedigree dog. By careful selection of your puppy from healthy tested parents, you will have the best chance to have a dog which will have a healthy life. Nevertheless, it is important that all Golden Retriever owners are aware of the potential diseases and are proactive in seeking veterinary advice if any of the symptoms become apparent.

CHAPTER 13
Working

"Most people might not realize the breed truly is a working breed, in that retrieving is genetically ingrained and that this innate quality proves time and time again that training a retriever with the reward of fetch is about as golden as it gets."

Gina Carr
Brier Golden Retrievers

The Golden Retriever's innate intelligence and trainability means that this is a breed ideally suited to working in a wide variety of situations. It is a credit to the adaptability of the breed that you may find Golden Retrievers working in all walks of life, in the field, in the home, in urban settings, at ports and airports. Dogs that find their vocation in working alongside their humans are usually carefully selected at birth and highly trained from an early age, although in certain circumstances, their potential may be spotted in a shelter. Although this book is primarily focused on companion animals, it is worth acknowledging just how capable and adaptable the Golden Retriever is by looking at some of the areas in which he may be found at work.

Photo Courtesy of Heather Dawson

Field Work

The Golden Retriever was originally bred as a hunting dog, as explained in Chapter 2. The breed was developed for its stamina, trainability, soft mouth, and the ability to work over terrain pocketed with marshes and streams. Today, these working characteristics are usually secondary in importance to the even-tempered, friendly nature of the Golden Retriever as a companion dog, and the breed has shown a divergence. Those planning to use a Golden Retriever in the field will be looking specifically for working lines. Dogs from these lines may prove too energetic to fit the mold of placid family dog. In fact, they may even find themselves in rescue if they have been taken on inadvertently by an owner looking for a pet, subsequently finding themselves with more of a handful than they bargained for. So, it is possible to find a working Golden Retriever in a shelter, but he is unlikely to have had the early gundog training to prepare him for being a hunting dog if he was given up very early. In experienced hands, however, he may still find his vocation.

Photo Courtesy of
Julie & Holly Simmons
PrairieWyn Golden Retrievers

In practice, Golden Retrievers have been rather overshadowed in the field by their Labrador cousins. One disadvantage to the breed is their long coat, which is much higher maintenance in wet muddy conditions than the Labrador's short coat. They may also be less prevalent as they can cost more than a Labrador. But the most likely explanation is that the Golden Retriever has proven such an outstanding success as a companion dog, that breeders are concentrating on producing the more placid lines and working lines are a bit of a specialty.

Golden Retrievers work differently in the field from Labradors. The Labrador is found with his nose to the ground following a scent, whereas the Golden Retriever acts on air scent and tends to carry their head up. They are known for their excellent game-finding ability and a unique elegance in the field that makes them favored very highly by experienced huntsmen.

If you have purchased a puppy from working stock with the intention to use him as a gundog, training will begin on a small scale from the day you bring him home. An early rapport will help to establish your partnership, ensuring the dog wants only to be with you. He needs to learn manners and trust. A strong bond will override fear, and ensure your dog will do your bidding and return to you in the field.

Formal gundog training should not start until the puppy is six or seven months so as not to "overcook" the dog's mind. At this stage they will learn to act on the whistle. Owners may choose to send their dog to gundog classes if they do not have prior experience, but the main priority must still be the partnership, so training cannot be fully delegated.

It's pretty amazing that the Golden Retriever has webbed feet! He is not quite a duck, but this breed trait comes from his water dog ancestors, and is an advantage to him working in wetland terrain.

Photo Courtesy of
David A Ring

Dogs for the Disabled

A dog that is individually trained to carry out tasks enabling a disabled person to have a more independent life is known as a service dog, or an assistance dog. The Golden Retriever is a very highly favored breed in this field because of their high intelligence and ability to learn, and the fact that they will do anything within their capabilities for their human. Golden Retrievers also thrive on using their brain.

The role most often associated with Golden Retrievers in the context of service dogs is as a guide dog for the blind. Not only can guide dogs help with tasks around the home, they have the important responsibility of keeping their owner safe out in public places. They also fulfill the vital role of companionship, as having a disability can feel very isolating, so the constant presence of a gentle-natured dog can help the disabled owner to face the challenges in their lives.

Guide dogs are bred from specialized breeding programs to ensure that the puppy will inherit the right character traits to be an assistance dog. They should be in excellent health, be confident and responsive, but remain focused and not distracted. At 8-10 weeks they will enter a training program until they are 12-18 months. They will be assessed during this time to see whether their future lies as a guide dog, a therapy dog, or a companion.

At 16-18 months, those that have been selected as guide dogs begin formal training, but during this time they also experience time out to play, go for walks, chew, and nap like any

Photo Courtesy of Meghan Shoeman

pet dog, as they will need to be comfortable in the home environment, however formal their training has been. At two years they will be paired with their new owner, who will themselves be trained for the new partnership. Golden Retrievers are also found as assistance dogs working alongside the deaf.

Dogs that do not go on to become guide dogs may find their vocation as therapy dogs. The qualities required of a therapy dog are a quiet and calm temperament and a friendly nature, so this role is ideally suited to a Golden Retriever. Therapy dogs interact with people to improve their emotional well-being. Studies have shown that playing with a dog can increase serotonin and dopamine, which promotes a feeling of contentment. Golden Retrievers are sometimes chosen as live-in therapy dogs, for example for people with autism; however, therapy dogs generally do not live with the person in need and are owned by a dedicated handler who takes the dog out to hospitals, nursing homes, and individual residences for short-term interaction. It is helpful, therefore, that the Golden Retriever loves everyone unconditionally, and is always ready to brighten the day of a total stranger.

An interesting fact is as an assistance dog, the Golden Retriever can be trained to turn lights on and off, open and close doors, and even load the washing machine!

Search and Rescue

Golden Retrievers excel as search and rescue (SAR) dogs, not only due to their trainability, eagerness to please, and steady temperament, but because they have an outstanding sense of smell. This makes them ideally suited for tracking in the event of a missing person, or a natural disaster where people may be buried under rubble or an avalanche. In these extreme conditions, their thick coat serves as protection. Golden Retrievers are the breed most often seen in

mass rescue situations, and it is claimed that they have the ability to do the work of 20-30 human beings. Search and rescue is always a race against the clock, so they really are the heroes of our time and have saved countless lives around the world.

Because Golden Retrievers are particularly adapted to picking up air-scents, they do not require a last-seen position, but can pick up human scent from anywhere in the area. They may be used to find victims that are still alive, or dead bodies by picking up decomposition gases. Golden Retrievers can even detect these in water. They are also used as evidence dogs by detecting items that have human scent on them, either from a living person, or the scent of a dead body.

To become a search and rescue dog, both the dog and handler have to go through rigorous training. Official search and rescue training cannot begin until the dog is fully grown at around 18 months, and takes between six months and two years. As with all working disciplines, the handler can begin the groundwork with their puppy in teaching obedience, trust, and establishing a bond.

Both handlers and dogs require national certification to participate in search and rescue, and this has to be renewed every few years.

Sometimes a shelter dog is talent spotted for a vocation in this field, and thereby in being rescued will go on to rescue others.

The Canadian Search Dog Association has the motto, Fide Canem, which means "Trust the Dog." This is the fundamental principle in search and rescue and the reason so many people owe their lives to a Golden Retriever.

Golden Retrievers have 300 million olfactory receptors in their noses, compared to a human, who only has 6 million. So, their sense of smell is 50 times greater than that of a human!

Police Dogs

Photo Courtesy of Melissa Morrison

As well as search and rescue, the Golden Retriever's sensitive nose makes him an asset to the police force, where his acute sense of smell can be trained to sniff out explosives and narcotics.

The Golden Retriever is not the breed most associated with police work; this honor falls to the German Shepherd, as a degree of natural aggression is required for protection duties, which the docile Golden Retriever does not possess. But on the other hand, apart from his excellent nose, the Golden Retriever has a desire to work and is quick to learn, building a connection with his handler, so that is why many Goldens earn the status of K9 as specialty detector dogs.

You will see Golden Retrievers at work in this field at airports, ports, and border crossings. Using their superior sense of smell, they will be trained to recognize explosives, firearms, illegal drugs, illegal imports such as animals or animal products, blood, currency, and even contraband electronics. It may seem miraculous enough that a dog's nose can pick out these items, but added to this, the detector dog can even identify them when they are masked by other odors, which smugglers will attempt in a futile bid to outsmart the nose of a Golden Retriever.

When the Golden Retriever detector dog picks up the target scent, he will signal to his handler by scratching at the surface near the source of the smell, or sitting near to it. The handler will be acutely attuned to the body language of his dog.

Typically, a detector dog can comprehensively examine a vehicle at a border in about 5 minutes, compared to the 20 minutes an officer without a dog would take to make a rudimentary search, so it goes without saying that as well as being more thorough, detector dogs keep traffic flowing and delays to a minimum at border crossings.

As with search and rescue, police detector dogs sometimes come from shelters. Some forces also have their own breeding programs. Dogs can be male or female and between 1 and 3 years to start work. Detector dogs will work an eight-hour day and their career will last up to eight years, after which they are usually adopted by their handler. Otherwise a good home will be found.

You may not know, causing intentional harm to or killing a police dog is a felony. If a K9 (police dog) is lost in the line of duty, they are buried with the same honors as their human partner.

As we have seen in this chapter, the Golden Retriever is an extremely versatile dog who will not only fit in with a family as a companion animal, but will excel in many different areas in the working world too.

CHAPTER 14
Breeding

Deciding about Breeding

The decision to breed your Golden Retriever should not be taken lightly. There are more puppies being produced in the world than loving homes, and with so many dogs in rescue shelters, it is not responsible to breed your dog just for fun, or because "it would be nice to have a litter." Breeding requires extensive knowledge, time, and money, so if you are looking at becoming a dedicated Golden Retriever breeder, then this chapter will give you some base knowledge to get you on your way. Breeding will not make you rich, but it can be extremely rewarding to contribute to improving the genetics of the Golden Retriever breed with a healthy, impressive litter of offspring.

Photo Courtesy of
Marnie Harrell – Shadymist Kennel, LLC

Photo Courtesy of
Lori Reuter – Avalor Goldens

Mating

Once you have decided that you are going to pursue mating your female Golden Retriever, you must first select a suitable mate. As mentioned in previous chapters, Golden Retrievers are prone to hip and elbow dysplasia as well as PRA, and therefore it is wise to select a sire to the puppies who has excellent hip and elbow scores, and has had genetic testing for ocular abnormalities. It is also prudent that you have invested in these tests for your dog too. Once you are sure that the match is one which will throw superb offspring, you must wait for your dog to have a season.

Female dogs will only be able to mate for several days during the time which their reproductive system is active, which is usually around 21 days. A dog will come into season every six months on average from the age of about one year old. However, it is important that the dog is allowed to have her first season before being mated. She can be mated between her second season up until five years old. After this, it is not recommended to breed as producing a litter of puppies requires the body to take on a great deal of strain, which an older body might not be able to handle.

Signs of a season include leaking pink-, red-, or brown-tinged liquid from the vulva, as well as swelling of that area too. It might be more

HELPFUL TIP
Genetic Testing

Since Golden Retrievers are prone to a variety of health problems, it's crucial to perform health tests on any dogs you plan to use for breeding. You should consider having the following organizations do these health tests on any breeding stock:

- The Canine Eye Registry Foundation does eye testing

- Auburn University tests for thrombopathia

- The Orthopedic Foundation for Animals (OFA) does the following tests: hip and elbow dysplasia, von Willebrand's disease, and hypothyroidism

swollen than usual, which can cause the dog to lick the area. In addition to this, most dogs will have a slight change in behavior, such as being clingier than usual or mothering toys. When she is actively in season, which will be for a few days within the 21-day cycle, she should visit the, stud dog. If she is ready, the stud dog will mount her to mate. He then turns around so they are facing away from each other. This is called a tie, and once tied, two dogs should not be forced apart, otherwise extensive damage can be done to the stud dog.

Pregnancy

When you think your dog might be pregnant, your vet will be able to investigate this for you. A blood test can be done at 22 days, and an ultrasound scan can be done at 42 days. Pregnancy lasts for a total of 63 days, and it is unlikely you will know how many puppies are in the mother until she gives birth. The only way is via an X-ray once the skeletons of the puppies have calcified, but X-rays can be dangerous for the development of a fetus.

When confirmed pregnant, the mother should not be placed under undue stress. Her body will be requiring more energy to fuel the growing puppies so feeding a high-quality diet is vital. She can still continue to go for walks; however, a 20-minute walk with minimal jumping and running is ideal. She must be provided with a warm, comfy place to rest throughout the day.

Toward the end of the pregnancy, you will start to notice her belly swelling and becoming hard. Her teats will also enlarge and she may appear hungrier than usual. She will also act more lethargic and start creating a nest with her soft toys if she has some.

Birthing

When the pregnancy is drawing to the end, it is a good idea to start measuring the mother's temperature. A normal temperature is between 101 and 102.5 degrees Fahrenheit, but when it drops, often to below 100 degrees Fahrenheit, then labor is likely to begin within the next 24 hours. When the mother goes into labor, she should be placed in a whelping box. This ensures she is giving birth in a safe environment for both her and the puppies. It can be homemade with a large cardboard box with one side cut down, or a hard dog bed can have the cushions taken out and lined with newspaper. This second option is the best as newspaper can be removed as it becomes soiled, and the bed is easy to clean down afterward.

Signs of labor include pacing, whining, and occasional pushing. It may go on for quite some time, but this is normal. Puppies are not passed all at once and there can be up to two hours between delivery of puppies. The puppies will come out inside the amniotic sac, which the mother will rip open, but occasionally it might break in the birth canal. The mother then will turn around to the puppy and lick it to clean away the amniot-

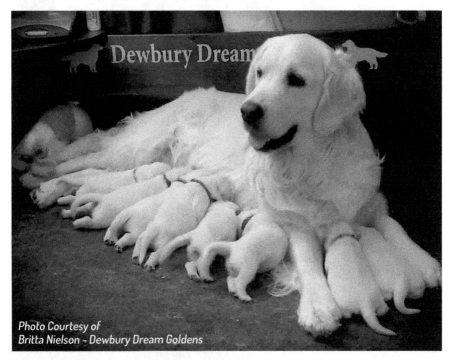

Photo Courtesy of
Britta Nielson - Dewbury Dream Goldens

Photo Courtesy of
Angel Martin - Goldensglen

ic fluid and warm up the pup. Some breeders prefer to pick up the puppy once it has been born, and rub it on the back vigorously with a towel to dry it. This will stimulate breathing, and is beneficial if the mother is a first-time mother and not showing very good instincts, but is generally not necessary. The breeder will usually check the nose and mouth to make sure it is clear of fluid as well.

If the mother's temperature drops and there have been no puppies in the past 24 hours, she seems in excruciating pain, she's straining unproductively, there has not been a puppy passed within two hours of the last and it is known that there are more in there, or she is producing green discharge, she should be taken to the emergency veterinarian as she may need a cesarean section. Time is of the essence as the sooner she has the surgery, the higher the chance that the puppies will survive.

Once all the puppies have arrived, the mother will eat the amniotic sacs and umbilical cords. While this doesn't sound appetizing to us, it provides her with a boost of nutrients to get her milk production underway. She should then be allowed to rest and nurse in a warm place (85 degrees Fahrenheit) without a breeze with her puppies, to allow them to suckle. They shouldn't be placed on a soft dog bed as this increases the chances that they might become smothered.

Aftercare

The birth is tiring, so allow the mother and puppies to rest following the birth. The mother can be given a warm sponge bath to clean up any mess from the birth, once she has had time to have a rest, and then given food and water. She probably won't want to eat immediately, but she should have food and water available to her for when she is ready.

For approximately a week after giving birth, there might be some slight discharge from the vulva of the mother. A light pink, red, or brown color is normal, but if it is fetid in odor or black or green then she must be immediately seen by a vet.

A few days after birth, it is a good idea to take the mother and puppies to your local veterinarian. This way he can examine them all to ensure they are in prime health, and that the puppies are not suffering from cleft palates, heart murmurs, or umbilical hernias.

Raising Puppies

It is exciting to have a litter of puppies grow up in your house, and even more exciting to start finding their potential homes. It is your responsibility that the future homes of the puppies are experienced and loving, and there is nothing wrong with vetting the new owners. Potential buyers will come to your house to view the puppies. They can do this from a young age and may choose to reserve one until you are happy for them to be released. Most breeders will then put a collar on the puppy which can distinguish it from the rest, unless the puppy has a distinctive marking.

Photo Courtesy of
Lori Reuter – Avalor Goldens

The puppies can go to their new homes from eight weeks old, but some breeders choose to keep the puppy until 12 weeks. At around four weeks old, they might start nibbling on their mother's food in addition to nursing. They can start to be offered some puppy food at this age, although they probably will only manage wet food, or soaked kibble. Over the following four weeks, they will gradually wean onto the puppy food exclusively.

Puppies need to be wormed against roundworms at 2, 4, 6, 8, and 12 weeks of age as they are particularly susceptible at a young age to pick up worms. They only need to have flea treatment if they have fleas, and if they need to be treated, they should be done so with a product which is suitable for puppies, as many flea products cannot be used on very young or very small animals. Some breeders will include a microchip and first vaccination of the initial vaccination course in the cost of the puppy, and this can be done at eight weeks old by a veterinarian. If the puppy has not yet been reserved, then the microchip will need to be registered to the breeder, and then the details changed when it is sold.

A litter of Golden Retrievers will bring you bundles of joy and fun, and it can be extremely rewarding to know you are contributing to improving the genetics of the breed, especially if you have bred close to the breed standard. However, breeding puppies is not easy, and it takes considerable knowledge and finances, so if you are not familiar with breeding and not planning to breed commercially, it is best to leave it up to the professional registered Golden Retriever breeders out there.

CHAPTER 15
Showing

Selecting a Dog for Showing

The overall American Kennel Club (AKC) breed standard for the Golden Retriever is quite lengthy, but the dog's general appearance should be like this: "A symmetrical, powerful, active dog, sound and well put together, not clumsy nor long in the leg, displaying a kindly expression and possessing a personality that is eager, alert, and self-confident. Primarily a hunting dog, he should be shown in hard working condition. Overall appearance, balance, gait, and purpose to be given more emphasis than any of his component parts. Any departure from the described ideal shall be considered faulty to the degree to which it interferes with the breed's purpose or is contrary to breed character."

The Golden Retriever is a stunning-looking breed and it is not surprising that many owners wish to showcase the beauty of their dog by entering him or her in competitions. Of course, the level at which the owner may wish to show their dog is a matter of personal preference. Local fun dog shows will be a much less pressurized environment where greater leeway may be permitted in the breed standard. But owners wishing to progress to national shows will need to familiarize themselves with the breed standard in their country before selecting a puppy, and research the genetics of the different lines that have puppies for sale. Success in the show ring begins with correct conformation, which means conforming to the ideal. This ideal may not be the same in every country, so if you select a puppy that deviates too far from the breed standard, progression beyond local shows will never happen, however beautiful the dog.

The first consideration when selecting a puppy is whether you wish to show a male or female dog. This is a matter of personal preference that may also be influenced by whether you intend to breed from your dog. Both sexes can excel in the show ring, although females have a season twice a year that can cause them to drop their coat, which will be disadvantageous if the show date coincides. Both sexes, however, should display the same attributes of correct conformation, confidence, patience, and adaptability, as well as graceful movement and the ability to stand still. Some of these attributes, such as confidence, may be observed amongst a litter of puppies, and others, such as conformation, may be assessed in combination with consideration of the parents, both of whom should be seen. Other attributes will need to be taught. This is why the owner who is serious about showing their Golden Retriever will almost always do best to select a puppy, as unless an adult dog comes from a showing background, he or she will not have the early training for success.

If you are already an experienced Golden Retriever owner or have a longstanding interest in the breed, you may already know which lines you are interested in, and will be registering your interest with the breeders in preparation for forthcoming litters. If you are new to the breed, you may obtain a list of approved breeders from the Kennel Club in your country. In order to show your dog, both parents will need to be registered, as will your puppy, which the breeder will do for the whole litter. Buying a puppy from an unregistered breeder will disqualify the dog from anything other than fun, local shows, as the purpose of high-level showing is to showcase the ideal genetic lines for the perpetuation of optimum standards in future generations. This is in the interest of the health and welfare of the breed, so observance of the rules has a humane objective.

So, you have identified a breeder who has a litter of puppies that will be ready to go at 8-10 weeks. How early can you pick out your future show champion? The answer is at around five weeks of age, and as previously discussed in Chapter 4, you will be looking for a healthy pup that is bright and alert and happy to be handled, but for the show ring you will have some additional considerations. Your chosen pup should not be expected to reach an adult size outside of the breed standard range. Consideration of the size of the parents should be an indicator of this. It should not have any unusual markings, pigmentation anomalies, or conformation faults such as an undershot or overshot bite, and although his or her coloration will be lighter as a puppy than its adult coat, extreme shades should be avoided. It may seem harsh, but these puppies will find loving homes as pets where showing is not an owner priority. Remember also that the breeder is an expert and will help guide your choice. Maintaining a relationship with the breeder will have the mutual benefit that he or she can follow the successes of their offspring in the show ring, and you will have a mentor from whom you can learn as your dog progresses.

After Selecting Your Puppy

Photo Courtesy of Deb Litzelfelner

So, having done your research, you have selected your future show champion and reserved him or her for collection when ready to leave the mother. At this stage, the dog is registered to the breeder. When you collect your puppy, the breeder will give you the Kennel Club Registration Information Document so you can change the registered ownership into your name. You will not be able to show your dog until this has been done, so it makes sense to organize it right away. This can be done by post or online, and you will then have the additional support and resources of the Kennel Club which will be invaluable for showing.

The most important priority for your young puppy if he is to do well in the show ring is socialization. Your dog is going to need to be comfortable around humans and all the other dogs in the show environment. Hopefully you have already picked out a confident dog, but socialization with other dogs needs to begin as soon as he has completed his first vaccinations, and with humans from the day he is born. Normal puppy socialization and training classes will put the basics into place, but in addition to this, your show dog needs to learn to be handled by strangers, to stand still, and to tolerate being "stacked" or put into the right position for the judge. He will have to learn to move to his best advantage. His carefully selected genetics should be the foundation for this, but learning to utilize his most graceful gait for the show ring is a desired objective for both dog and handler.

There is no better way to learn the techniques for showing your dog than to visit shows and observe. Bringing your young dog with you will also accustom him to the showing environment before any expectations are placed upon him. You will both be learning together and will be ready to hit the ground running when you enter your first show after the puppy has reached the required six months of age. You may also get to meet experienced breeders and handlers and pick up some tips firsthand. Knowing what to expect will make the initial stages of your dog's show career considerably less daunting. You will also get to appreciate the qualities that make a show champion, and assess your own dog's strengths and weaknesses against the breed standard. You will observe show etiquette and how to manage disappointment and the dignified acceptance of what you may consider a wrong decision. You will be ready to show your dog to its best advantage from the get-go, and maybe pick up some early ribbons to encourage you along the way.

It should be noted that the historical expectation of show dogs is that they should be entire, and whereas neutering is recommended for pet dogs, you will not be able to show a neutered dog in high-level conformation competitions in the USA. This is because the purpose of conformation showing is to prove that a dog is worthy of being bred from. In the UK, exemptions are granted upon application for a permission to show letter from the Kennel Club. However, it is acknowledged that spaying makes the coat coarser in female dogs, and in practice, the absence of testicles in the male dog may influence the judge's decision when allocating the higher placings.

Breed Standards

It is vitally important to acknowledge that the breed standard for the Golden Retriever differs from country to country, and your dog needs to conform to the standard in the country in which he or she is competing. It has already been observed that the American Golden Retriever is darker and lankier than the pale, squarer-set British Golden Retriever. Conformation shows are about nothing other than the alignment with the desired breed standard in a particular country, so this has to be the most important resource you need for showing your dog. The standards for the USA and the UK are given here. Elsewhere you should consult the Kennel Club for your country, but breed standards are easily found online.

The American Kennel Club (USA)
Official Standard for the Golden Retriever (1990)

General Appearance: A symmetrical, powerful, active dog, sound and well put together, not clumsy nor long in the leg, displaying a kindly expression and possessing a personality that is eager, alert and self-confident. Primarily a hunting dog, he should be shown in hard working condition. Overall appearance, balance, gait and purpose to be given more emphasis than any of his component parts. Faults - Any departure from the described ideal shall be considered faulty to the degree to which it interferes with the breed's purpose or is contrary to breed character.

Size, Proportion, Substance: Males 23 to 24 inches in height at withers; females 21½ to 22½ inches. Dogs up to one inch above or below stan-

*Photo Courtesy of
Jill Simmons
PoeticGold Farm*

dard size should be proportionately penalized. Deviation in height of more than one inch from the standard shall disqualify. Length from breastbone to point of buttocks slightly greater than height at withers in ratio of 12:11. Weight for male dogs 65 to 75 pounds; female dogs 55 to 65 pounds.

Head: Broad in skull, slightly arched laterally and longitudinally without prominence of frontal bones (forehead) or occipital bones. Stop well defined but not abrupt. Foreface deep and wide, nearly as long as skull. Muzzle straight in profile, blending smooth and strongly into skull; when viewed in profile or from above, slightly deeper and wider at stop than at tip. No heaviness in flews. Removal of whiskers is permitted but not preferred. Eyes friendly and intelligent in expression, medium large with dark, close-fitting rims, set well apart and reasonably deep in sockets. Color preferably dark brown; medium brown acceptable. Slant eyes and narrow, triangular eyes detract from correct expression and are to be faulted. No white or haw visible when looking straight ahead. Dogs showing evidence of functional abnormality of eyelids or eyelashes (such as, but not limited to, trichiasis, entropion, ectropion, or distichiasis) are to be excused from the ring. Ears rather short with front edge attached well behind and just above the eye and falling close to cheek. When pulled forward, tip of ear should just cover the eye. Low, hound-like ear set to be faulted. Nose black or brownish black, though fading to a lighter shade in cold weather not serious. Pink nose or one seriously lacking in pigmentation to be faulted. Teeth scissors bite, in which the outer side of the lower incisors touches the inner side of the upper incisors. Undershot or overshot bite is a disqualification. Misalignment of teeth (irregular placement of incisors) or a level bite (incisors meet each other edge to edge) is undesirable, but not to be confused with undershot or overshot. Full dentition. Obvious gaps are serious faults.

Neck, Topline, Body: Neck medium long, merging gradually into well laid-back shoulders, giving sturdy, muscular appearance. No throatiness. Backline strong and level from withers to slightly sloping croup, whether standing or moving. Sloping backline, roach or sway back, flat or steep croup to be faulted. Body well balanced, short coupled, deep through the chest. Chest between forelegs at least as wide as a man's closed hand including thumb, with well-developed forechest. Brisket extends to elbow. Ribs long and well sprung but not barrel shaped, extending well towards hindquarters. Loin short, muscular, wide and deep, with very little tuck-up. Slabsidedness, narrow chest, lack of depth in brisket, excessive tuck-up to be faulted. Tail well set on, thick and muscular at the base, following the natural line of the croup. Tail bones extend to, but not below, the point of hock. Carried with merry action, level or with some moderate upward curve; never curled over back nor between legs.

Forequarters: Muscular, well-coordinated with hindquarters and capable of free movement. Shoulder blades long and well laid back with upper tips fairly close together at withers. Upper arms appear about the same length as the blades, setting the elbows back beneath the upper tip of the blades, close to the ribs without looseness. Legs, viewed from the front, straight with good bone, but not to the point of coarseness. Pasterns short and strong, sloping slightly with no suggestion of weakness. Dewclaws on forelegs may be removed, but are normally left on. Feet medium size, round, compact, and well knuckled, with thick pads. Excess hair may be trimmed to show natural size and contour. Splayed or hare feet to be faulted.

Hindquarters: Broad and strongly muscled. Profile of croup slopes slightly; the pelvic bone slopes at a slightly greater angle (approximately 30 degrees from horizontal). In a natural stance, the femur joins the pelvis at approximately a 90-degree angle; stifles well bent; hocks well let down with short, strong rear pasterns. Feet as in front. Legs straight when viewed from rear. Cow-hocks, spread hocks, and sickle hocks to be faulted.

Coat: Dense and water-repellent with good undercoat. Outer coat firm and resilient, neither coarse nor silky, lying close to body; may be straight or wavy. Untrimmed natural ruff; moderate feathering on back of forelegs and on underbody; heavier feathering on front of neck, back of thighs and underside of tail. Coat on head, paws, and front of legs is short and even. Excessive length, open coats, and limp, soft coats are very undesirable. Feet may be trimmed and stray hairs neatened, but the natural appearance of coat or outline should not be altered by cutting or clipping.

Color: Rich, lustrous golden of various shades. Feathering may be lighter than rest of coat. With the exception of graying or whitening of face or body due to age, any white marking, other than a few white hairs on the chest, should be penalized according to its extent. Allowable light shadings are not to be confused with white markings. Predominant body color which is either extremely pale or extremely dark is undesirable. Some latitude should be given to the light puppy whose coloring shows promise of deepening with maturity. Any noticeable area of black or other off-color hair is a serious fault.

Gait: When trotting, gait is free, smooth, powerful and well-coordinated, showing good reach. Viewed from any position, legs turn neither in nor out, nor do feet cross or interfere with each other. As speed increases, feet tend to converge toward center line of balance. It is recommended that dogs be shown on a loose lead to reflect true gait.

Temperament: Friendly, reliable, and trustworthy. Quarrelsomeness or hostility towards other dogs or people in normal situations, or an unwarranted show of timidity or nervousness, is not in keeping with Golden Retriever character. Such actions should be penalized according to their significance.

Disqualifications: Deviation in height of more than one inch from standard either way. Undershot or overshot bite.

The Kennel Club of Great Britain (UK)
Official Standard for the Golden Retriever (1994)

General Appearance: Symmetrical, balanced, active, powerful, level mover; sound with kindly expression.

Characteristics: Biddable, intelligent and possessing natural working ability.

Temperament: Kindly, friendly and confident.

Head and Skull: Balanced and well chiseled, skull broad without coarseness; well set on neck, muzzle powerful, wide and deep. Length of foreface approximately equals length from well-defined stop to occiput. Nose preferably black.

Eyes: Dark brown, set well apart, dark rims.

Ears: Moderate size, set on approximate level with eyes.

Mouth: Jaws strong, with a perfect, regular and complete scissor bite, i.e. upper teeth closely overlapping lower teeth and set square to the jaws.

Neck: Good length, clean and muscular.

Forequarters: Forelegs straight with good bone, shoulders well laid back, long in blade with upper arm of equal length placing legs well under body. Elbows close fitting.

Body: Balanced, short-coupled, deep through heart. Ribs deep, well sprung. Level topline.

Hindquarters: Loin and legs strong and muscular, good second thighs, well bent stifles. Hocks well let down, straight when viewed from rear, neither turning in nor out. Cow-hocks highly undesirable.

Feet: Round and cat-like.

Tail: Set on and carried level with back, reaching to hocks, without curl at tip.

Gait/Movement: Powerful with good drive. Straight and true in front and rear. Stride long and free with no sign of hackney action in front.

Coat: Flat or wavy with good feathering, dense water-resisting undercoat.

Color: Any shade of gold or cream, neither red nor mahogany. A few white hairs on chest only, permissible.

Size: Height at withers: dogs: 56-61 cms (22-24 ins); bitches: 51-56 cms (20-22 ins).

Faults: Any departure from the foregoing points should be considered a fault and the seriousness with which the fault should be regarded should be in exact proportion to its degree and its effect upon the health and welfare of the dog and on the dog's ability to perform its traditional work.

Note: Male animals should have two apparently normal testicles fully descended into the scrotum.

Photo Courtesy of Angel Martin Goldensglen

Preparing for a Show

Showing your dog in conformation classes can take place locally and informally, or on the tightly regulated, prestigious Kennel Club circuit. However, you will probably wish to start in a low-pressure setting so that you and your dog can get a feel for showing and enjoy the experience. There may even be novelty classes at local shows, where all the rules are thrown out the window, and you and your dog can really have fun.

However, you have selected and trained your Golden Retriever for high-level success, so you will soon want to move up the rankings and compete with the best. In registering your puppy with the Kennel Club and joining the Golden Retriever Club in your country, you will have access to show listings, and be able to plan ahead for the shows you would like to enter. Be sure to send your application and payment off in good time, then you can start planning for the big day.

If the show you are entering is some distance away, you may also wish to consider booking dog-friendly accommodations near the venue, so your dog has time to settle, especially if he or she suffers from travel stress or sickness.

Your Golden Retriever's coat is its crowning glory, and naturally you wish it to look its best on the day. If you are showing a female dog, it is wise not to choose a show near to her season, as shedding will affect the quality of her coat. Remember that the breed standard looks for a natural appearance, so you should not have your dog clipped or unnaturally barbered. You will need to be grooming your dog on a daily basis to maintain the natural silkiness of the coat and distribution of the oils. If you wish to bathe your dog, this should be done a few days before the show to enable the natural oils to return to the coat by show day. Be aware that although certain grooming tricks may disguise minor conformation faults at a glance, the judge is experienced and will be thoroughly examining the dog with their hands, so they will not be fooled by any fluffing and thinning over problem areas.

As part of your dog's regular grooming routine, you should be cleaning their teeth daily, as missing or decayed teeth will constitute a fault in the show ring.

You will have been practicing stacking your dog for the judge, maintaining his attention, and working on his optimum pace to demonstrate his fluid gait. These things will only improve with experience. Baiting is usually permitted in the ring to bring a sparkle to the eye of your dog at the right moment; however, overuse of food treats will not impress the judge. At all times in the ring, whether standing or moving, consider the outline of the dog, especially the side profile. As the handler, be sure to wear a neutral or dark plain color to set your dog off to its best advantage against you, and practical shoes so that you are moving as effortlessly in the ring as your dog.

The judge is looking for the strengths of the dog, as all dogs will have some weaknesses—none are perfect. Remember, although they are measuring the dog against the breed standard, to a certain extent the final placings will be a matter of opinion, and you may not agree. Good sportsmanship in competition is considered the correct showing etiquette, and you should never question the judge's decision. There will always be another day!

This chapter has discussed conformation showing; however, the Golden Retriever is a dog of many talents and may compete in other disciplines, such as agility, flyball, obedience, gundog events, and working trials. For these classes, it will not matter if the dog has cosmetic faults or has been neutered. There will always be an arena in which your Golden Retriever may shine, and he will relish the opportunity to stimulate his active brain, building the bond between you both as you bring in the ribbons together.

CHAPTER 16
Living with a Senior Dog

It is inevitable that at some point in your journey as a Golden Retriever owner, your furry friend will reach his twilight years. If you've had your dog since a puppy, this might seem a long way off, whereas if you adopted an older dog, then maybe those years are coming up soon. Nevertheless, aging is an inevitable fact of life, and it must not be put to one side. Age is only a number, and therefore it doesn't mean that your Golden is going to become ancient and ill at the age of eight or nine; however, older dogs are more predisposed to certain ailments, and this chapter will provide you with an overview of what to expect, and how to prevent these things from happening.

Photo Courtesy of Kelly Kelly

Diet

The first thing to start with when your dog is becoming a little older is to change him gradually onto a senior food. This can be done over the course of a week, as discussed earlier in the book. A food specific to senior dogs is vital, as it provides different quantities of nutrients from puppy or adult food, which are more suitable for an older dog.

Senior dog foods may have slightly fewer calories than food for younger dogs. This is because older dogs are usually more sedentary, and therefore need less calories to see them through the day. An overweight older dog will have extra strain on his vital organs, which may not be functioning at full capacity any more, and will work better if there is not a layer of fat surrounding them.

HELPFUL TIP
Accommodating a Senior Dog

Senior Golden Retrievers (those over the age of seven) need special considerations in your home. Since Goldens are prone to joint problems like hip dysplasia and arthritis, senior Goldens benefit from things like orthopedic dog beds and rubber booties if their feet slip on your hard floors. If your Golden starts losing his sight due to cataracts or other eye conditions, try to avoid moving any furniture and keep your dog's main walking paths clear.

This type of food is also usually focused on joint health and mobility. As we will discuss later in this chapter, Golden Retrievers often struggle with their mobility later in life, and thus need an extra bit of help. Senior foods are usually composed of ingredients which are high in omega fatty acids. These are excellent natural anti-inflammatories for aching joints. They also work to improve the quality and viscosity of the joint fluid to ensure the joints are well lubricated.

The final aspects about senior dog food which might be different from regular food, are the concentrations of nutrients such as sodium, potassium, calcium, and phosphorus. These affect the health of the kidneys and too much or too little of them may put extra strain on the kidneys. Therefore, having exactly the right amount in the food will ensure that the kidneys do not need to work too hard—something many older dogs' kidneys cannot cope with.

Senior Wellness Checks

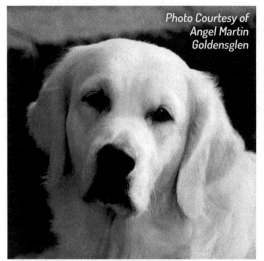

Photo Courtesy of Angel Martin Goldensglen

To ensure your senior Golden is kept in top health, senior wellness checks from your vet are recommended. This is in addition to your usual annual vaccination check. The reason for these checks is to ensure anything which is deteriorating is picked up very early in the course of disease. That way it can be treated as soon as possible and the progression slowed.

A senior wellness check will start with a physical exam. Your vet will check the head area first, the teeth for any excessive tartar, and the eyes for any cloudiness. Next, he will listen to the heart and lungs to make sure the heart is beating in a regular rhythm and that the lungs are clear and not wheezing. Finally, he will feel the abdomen for any lumps as well as the size of the liver. He might try to feel the kidneys, but in larger dogs such as Golden Retrievers, they can be extremely hard to feel unless the dog is very thin.

After the clinical exam, your vet will probably take some blood to check for general organ health. The blood is usually taken from the jugular vein in the neck, but some vets prefer the cephalic vein in the front leg. A small patch of hair will be clipped so the vet can see the vein and make the procedure as quick as possible for your Golden. This blood test will give a good indication of the internal health of your dog and pick up on any very early stage problems.

Finally, your vet may also perform a blood pressure test. This is much like a blood pressure test in a human, where a cuff is placed around the front leg and inflated. This is then deflated and the vet will investigate at what pressure the pulse returns further down the leg. Older dogs may be prone to higher blood pressure due to kidney or heart disease, and early detection will enable your dog to receive medication for it.

Arthritis

As discussed in Chapter 12, Golden Retrievers are prone to joint diseases such as hip dysplasia and elbow dysplasia. Arthritis will develop in any joint which either is normal, but with abnormal forces on it, or an abnormal joint with normal forces on it. Hip and elbow dysplasia are abnormal joints and unfortunately, developing arthritis is the natural progression in the course of the disease.

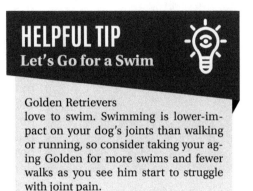

HELPFUL TIP
Let's Go for a Swim

Golden Retrievers love to swim. Swimming is lower-impact on your dog's joints than walking or running, so consider taking your aging Golden for more swims and fewer walks as you see him start to struggle with joint pain.

The main signs of arthritis are limping and feeling crunching when flexing and extending the joint. The reason this happens is because the smooth cartilage which lines the ends of the bones in the joint has started to deteriorate. Therefore, the joints tend to have a grating action when they move, rather than a smooth gliding action.

Once the cartilage has been destroyed, unfortunately there is nothing that can be done to regenerate it. However, there are ways of slowing down the degeneration process. The first way, which should be applied from a young age in active dogs, or dogs with joint conditions, is by adding a joint supplement to the diet. These joint supplements almost always contain glucosamine, but may also contain chondroitin and green-lipped mussel. Joint supplements stimulate the synthesis of proteoglycans, which are the main components of cartilage. They also improve the health of the joint fluid, ensuring it is thick and plenteous in volume so that the joint can move easily. Joint supplements can come in many forms, such as tablets, capsules, treats, powders, or even already combined into a senior food.

The next way which will aid in maintaining the health of the joint is to keep your dog slim. An overweight dog will have increased pressure on these joints, which in turn will cause them to deteriorate faster. If you have an older dog with reduced mobility, and increasing his exercise is not an option, putting him on a diet will be beneficial to him. This can either be through giving him less of his regular food, or giving him a satiety food, which is bulky and will enable him to feel fuller for longer. However, if you wish to increase his exercise, but don't want to put extra stress on the joints, then hydrotherapy is an excellent option to consider. Your Golden is bound to love it since they are generally drawn to water.

Photo Courtesy of Meghan Shoeman

If your vet feels that your dog's quality of life is becoming compromised by the pain of arthritis, which is evident in any dog which is limping, he may prescribe some pain medications for him. Most dogs will have prescribed a non-steroidal anti-inflammatory drug (NSAID) as the first pain relief medication to try. Some dogs have a slightly sensitive gut on NSAIDs, but do not worry, there are plenty of other medications to try if your dog does not respond well to NSAIDs.

If you wish to try a method of pain relief which does not involve drugs, some vets offer acupuncture to their patients. This stimulates the release of endorphins, which are the body's natural pain relief.

Dementia

As dogs age, so does their brain, and therefore so does their mentation. It is now a recognized problem that some dogs suffer from canine cognitive dysfunction (CCD). This is a very similar deterioration of the brain as dementia in humans.

The most common sign you will notice in your dog with CCD is dullness, but also with that may come aimless wandering, urinating or defecating in the house when he was previously house trained, and behavior changes.

CCD cannot be reversed; however, your veterinarian will be able to provide a very safe daily medication which improves the blood flow to the brain. This in turn increases the oxygen flow and the ability of the brain to process things much better. Owners often find it gives their dog a whole new lease on life.

Organ Deterioration

As previously mentioned, the kidneys and liver in particular are the most susceptible organs to deterioration later on in life. This is because these organs are very sensitive to changes in blood pressure, diet, toxin ingestion, medications, and general lifestyle throughout the dog's life.

Early detection with senior wellness blood tests will ensure that you are aware of any issues early on so that basic lifestyle changes can be made to stop deterioration further. Diet changes, in particular, can take a lot of the strain off the kidneys and organs, and some of the top veterinary brand dog foods sell diets specifically for liver or kidney diseased patients. Liver diets have a lower amount of protein, but the protein that it has is of higher quality than normal dog foods. The liver has to convert the protein into a more usable form, so this means it doesn't have to work so hard. Kidney diets have different amounts of minerals, as mentioned earlier, which are filtered by the kidneys.

Photo Courtesy of Debbie & Michael Seybert

If the liver disease cannot be managed by diet, an ultrasound guided biopsy might be taken to understand exactly what is wrong with it, although in older dogs it is usually liver fibrosis or liver cancer which is the main problem. This can be done under sedation, as while it is not extremely painful, it is a long needle and if the dog were to move, then it could cause significant harm. If the liver disease cannot be treated directly, for example with chemotherapy for cancer, then supportive liver medications can be prescribed to your dog such as SAM-e or ursodeoxycholic acid. These improve liver function.

Kidney disease, on the other hand, can be managed in many ways. An ultrasound of the kidneys will usually be done to understand whether there is an underlying cause of the kidney disease, such as cysts or tumors, or whether it is just chronic deterioration which happens with age. When kidneys deteriorate, many bodily functions are impacted. These include the production of red blood cells, so the dog may become anemic, the regulation of blood pressure, so the dog may have high blood pressure, and the filtration of water and waste products, so the dog may urinate more. There are drugs available to help with all of these issues, but sometimes if the kidneys have become advanced in the disease process, some time spent on intravenous fluids may improve things.

Loss of Senses

The classical picture of an elderly dog is one which is deaf or blind. Losing these senses is very common and should be anticipated while your dog still has all his senses intact.

When your dog can still hear well, teach hand commands as well as voice commands. These have been discussed in Chapter 6.

The eyes may unfortunately deteriorate at the same time though. Cloudy eyes are normal in older dogs, and are not a sign that he can't see. A normal condensation of the fibers within the lens is called nuclear sclerosis, and this the dog can still see through. Cataracts can look very similar to nuclear sclerosis, but the main difference is that dogs cannot see through cataracts. A veterinarian can differentiate between cataracts and nuclear sclerosis by shining a bright light in the eye. If he can then see to the back of the eye, it is nuclear sclerosis, whereas if the light reflects back off the lens, then it is a cataract. These can be removed, but due to the age at which they normally develop, many owners opt not to go through with the operation due to the increased risk of the anesthetic.

Bladder Control

If you have a female Golden, and she was spayed before her first season, then you might start having issues with her leaking small amounts of urine. She isn't aware she's doing this, and is not purposely urinating in her bed or on the floor, so do not scold her for it.

When the urethral sphincter (the tight muscular band which holds closed the exit to the bladder) has not had any influence from estrogen during its lifetime, then it is significantly weaker than it should be. This results in it becoming leaky when pressure is put on the abdomen and therefore the bladder, for example lying down.

It can be managed well with a couple of drug options. These come in syrup and tablet forms and must be given daily. If the urine leakage is excessive, you may need to keep the long hair around the bottom area trimmed, so that the area stays clean and doesn't lead to urine scald.

Saying Goodbye

For many owners, there will come a time when you have to make a decision whether it is in your dog's best interests to be put to sleep, otherwise known as euthanized. It is not often the case that a sudden bout of illness will take your dog, but in the elderly years it is usually a chronic and slow disease which will cause his welfare to be compromised. For our animals, we have the ability to decide whether their quality of life is so significantly compromised that they should not carry on.

While this is obviously devastating for us as owners, a dog has no negative feelings about being euthanized and it is a gentle and pain-free procedure. A dog cannot comprehend or anticipate what is going to happen like we can as humans. When a dog is put to sleep, it is exactly that. The procedure is an overdose of anesthetic, which will make him slip into a deep sleep, where eventually his heart will stop. This can be done in a vet practice or at your home, whichever is better for you and your dog.

The injection is usually given in the cephalic vein in the leg. Your vet will probably put in a catheter to have constant access to the vein, as a large volume is usually needed for a Golden Retriever. Within seconds, your dog will fall asleep. Within 10-15 seconds the heart will have stopped, and your dog will have gently slipped away. You may notice some trembling or urination afterward, or what appears to be a deep breath, but these are all the signs of muscles contracting after death, and not signs that the injection hasn't worked.

It is always a very sad situation to say goodbye to your beloved friend; however, you must try to remember all of the amazing times your Golden has brought a smile to your face over the previous years, and look back on the time with fondness and gladness, rather than tears.

ACKNOWLEDGMENTS

Being a vet means that I get to see many different dogs, but amongst my favorites are definitely the Goldens. There's nothing better than to be greeted by a waggy tail and a great big grin. It was equally enjoyable to write this book on the breed. I hope it will win many people over to the breed! So, I'd like to thank my Golden Retriever patients and owners, who provided me with the excitement and motivation to write this book.

I would also like to thank my long-time book editor, Clare Hardy, who just has a way with words to make sure everything I write sounds fantastic. She's provided me with a great deal of support through all my writing efforts and it helps that she is a major dog lover too!